In His Hands, I Am Healed

Laura J. Weber

In His Hands, I am Healed

Laura J. Weber

Cover photo used by permission from Digital Mountain Media, Inc. (www.digitalmtnmedia.com)

Cover and interior design by Shaffer Creative, L.L.C. (www.shaffercreative.com)

ISBN 978-1-54394-303-0

Foreword by Ricky Texada for Laura Weber

When I first met Laura, I was struck by the deep humility that exuded from her. She gave my wife Cyd and me a short summary of her life's journey. No doubt Laura had many difficult experiences while growing up; each one had prepared her for the battles she would encounter as an adult.

There is an age-old question asked by many, "why do bad things happen to good people?" There is no simple answer to such a complex question. One thing is certain—we will all face trials as we traverse through the journey of life. Laura has learned much about what it takes to overcome the challenges confronted in the darkest of days.

What would you do if you were told that you had cancer? Would you curl up into a ball and refuse to fight? Would you descend into a deep dark hole of depression and despair? Or would you square your shoulders and firmly resolve in your mind to fight with every ounce of your being to conquer it? No doubt you would want to talk with someone who knows what it means to fight that dreadful disease and overcome.

Laura Weber is one person you would want in
your corner.

I'm so grateful that Laura has taken the time to write
this book. It is moving to see how she processed each
declaration of "you have cancer." You will witness
the resolve, courage, transparency and faith displayed
by Laura as she learns to lean into God. She shares
the promises made by God that helped her process
the emotions of worry, anxiety and fear. You will be
inspired observing the patience she demonstrated
while trusting God's timing to reveal Himself and His
word to her. Laura's focus on the Lord unveils a path
to which you can grow in your own faith as you deal
with adverse circumstances in your life. God's grace is
sufficient, His promises are true, and Laura's life is a
testimony trumpeting the truth of God's great love and
care for us all.

Ricky Texada, Campus Pastor
Covenant Church Colleyville

Table of Contents

Chapter 1
Being Grateful Through the Cancer

David and Goliath

The story of David and Goliath is one of my favorite Bible stories because it shows that l can have victory amid my storms regardless of how fierce they are.

1 Samuel 17-18 describes the story of how a young boy defeated Goliath, who tormented the armies of Israel to the point that they became dismayed and greatly afraid.

The Philistine armies stood on a mountain on one side, and Israel stood on a mountain on the other side, separated by a valley between them. For 40 days, Goliath, the champion of the Philistines, came out in the valley and tormented the Israelites with words and challenges to send a man to fight him. Goliath's rhetoric didn't deter David's belief that God would deliver the giant into his hands. David volunteered and said to Saul:

"Let no man's heart fail because of him; your servant will go and fight with this Philistine." 1 Samuel 17:32

Because David was a young boy, Saul initially told him that he couldn't go to fight Goliath (1 Samuel 17:33).

David reminded Saul how he killed lions and bears when they came to attack his father's sheep and said:

"The Lord, who delivered me from the paw of the lion and from the paw of the bear, He will deliver me from the hand of this Philistine." And Saul said to David, 'Go, and the Lord be with you!" 1 Samuel 17:37

Saul agreed to let David fight Goliath.

The battle between David and Goliath occurred in the valley. When David went out to meet the giant, there was an exchange of words between the two (1 Samuel 17:42-47).

"And when the Philistine looked about and saw David, he disdained him; for he was only a youth, ruddy and good-looking.

So the Philistine said to David, 'Am I a dog, that you come to me with sticks?' And the Philistine cursed David by his gods.

And the Philistine said to David, 'Come to me, and I will give your flesh to the birds of the air and the beasts of the field!'

Then David said to the Philistine, 'You come to me with a sword, with a spear, and with a javelin. But I come to you in the name of the Lord of hosts, the God of the armies of Israel, whom you have defied.

This day the Lord will deliver you into my hand, and I will strike you and take your head from you. And this day I will give the carcasses of the camp of the Philistines to the birds of the air and the wild beasts of the earth, that all the earth may know that there is a God in Israel.

Then all this assembly shall know that the Lord does not save with sword and spear; for the battle is the Lord's, and He will give you into our hands."

After an exchange of these words, David and Goliath ran toward each other and David killed Goliath with a sling and stone. The key to David's victory was his confidence that God would deliver Goliath into his hands.

David's unwavering faith is what we all need during our most challenging circumstances; getting this kind of unwavering faith can be a battle in and of itself.

I know the battle all too well.

A big storm struck my life in 2012. I was diagnosed with cancer. Little did I know then that I would hear the words "you have cancer" four more times after the original diagnosis.

My journey through cancer five times in 4 ½ years was like the story of David and Goliath. Cancer became my Goliath that screamed at and tormented me all the time, to the point that fear consumed and crippled me in 2015.

Although my world was turned upside down by the cancer Goliath that rushed into my life, I chose to be like David, trust God and meet it head on in the valley. In the end, God miraculously healed me and delivered me from my Goliath called cancer.

Laura's Journey Lesson
Being grateful for our journey through a valley allows us to gain an intimate knowledge about God that we otherwise wouldn't have had without the journey and valley.

As I share my own David and Goliath story in the following pages, I hope you will find encouragement and inspiration to face your own Goliath head-on as David did. As you read, you'll hear about my biggest struggles and how I overcame them. Additionally, you'll read about two critical decisions I made that resulted in a tectonic shift in my attitude and a question I asked God that saved my life: What must I do to be free? This led me to another question: What must I do to be healed? In both cases, God answered me, and His answer was simple – believe.

I am grateful for the journey through cancer because I've grown so much and gained an intimate knowledge of God that I wouldn't have otherwise had without the journey. Arriving at the place of totally believing that God would heal me and set me free from my cancer Goliath wasn't easy, but He did, and I'm so thankful for the journey. If you wish to know how you can reach this destination – being grateful for the journeys through your toughest storms and believing that God will set you free from them – then please read on.

Book's Organization

Chapters 2-6 describe my journey through each diagnosis. I also share "Laura's Journey Lessons" in each chapter that note the most significant lessons I learned while traveling through my journey with cancer.

I battled fear between my fourth and fifth diagnosis. I share how I achieved victory over fear in Chapter 7.

Cancer pushed me to Jesus. In the process of seeking Him, I found priceless treasures along the way that I share in Chapter 8. You will also find personal posts from a secret Facebook group that I set up the day after my original diagnosis; I describe this group in Chapter 2.

Chapter 9 provides medical evidence for my five diagnoses along with the evidence of my healing. An infographic showing the total timeline for the five diagnoses, surgeries, and treatments is presented. Individual infographics are presented on the first page of Chapters 2-6 to show my diagnosis, surgeries and treatments specific to each individual chapter.

Chapter 2
The Journey Begins

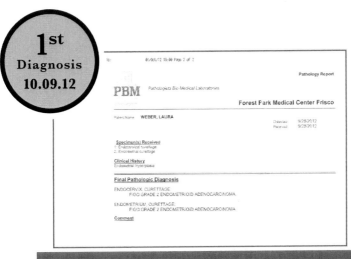

1st Diagnosis 10.09.12

Endometrial Adenocarcinoma

Treatment:
Surgery followed by 4 high dose radiation treatments

In September 2012, I saw a gynecologist for a routine appointment. He examined me and said he was concerned because my uterus was enlarged. He suggested I come back to have an ultrasound of the uterus. I came back a week later and had the ultrasound. After the ultrasound, the doctor scheduled me for a D&C because he was concerned with what he saw on the ultrasound. During the D&C, the doctor removed tissue from my uterus and sent it to a lab to be tested for cancer.

Because the doctor wasn't sure as to what was causing my uterus to be enlarged, he wasn't offering any speculation as to what could be the cause. That didn't matter to me. My inquiring mind wanted to know. I searched Google. I saw that uterine cancer was one of the possibilities. I remember thinking, "No, this can't be the cause," and I tried not to dwell on it too much. I kept telling myself to live with the information that I had to date and not let my mind wander off thinking about what it could be. I practiced this a lot in the two weeks while I waited for the results after my D&C.

October 9, 2012 – a day that forever changed my life. This was the day I first heard the words "you have cancer."

I remember feeling all calm on the outside, but shaking on the inside as my friend drove me to get the results from my D&C. Yes, I was afraid to hear the words "you have cancer," and these were words that I didn't want to hear. I heard them anyway. The doctor said it was Grade 2 uterine cancer. I never knew that cancers were graded. The doctor said that he was going to set up an appointment with the best gynecologist oncologist in the Dallas area and that their office would be getting in touch with me.

As I walked out of the doctor's office, my heart sank. The floodgates of tears poured out as I began to process that I was just diagnosed with cancer. All the feelings came rushing to me. Feelings of fear, bewilderment, and confusion overtook me. I felt so lost. I didn't know how to deal with these feelings. I managed to pull myself together because I realized I needed to call my mom and dad and share the news with them. This was difficult, but through all my feelings and tears, I managed to share the news in a semi-coherent way.

My friend and I stopped at a local marina and restaurant on Lewisville Lake in North Texas after we left the doctor's office. I asked her, "What does someone do after being diagnosed with cancer?" I asked her this question because she had recently lost her husband to cancer. She shared that she and her husband went home and built a screened-in porch after hearing the news. I wasn't gifted with carpentry skills so I knew I couldn't physically build anything. I had another friend who battled cancer a few years earlier tell me that she slept with her Bible the first night she found out.

I did sleep with my Bible the first night after receiving the news. I didn't sleep at all. It was more like drifting in and out of sleep. My mind kept flipping through my entire life's script. Nowhere did I find cancer in the script. I didn't know how to deal with it. I didn't know what to do. I felt so helpless and overwhelmed. Cancer invaded my life. There was no written script on how it would play out in my life. I was scared.

Laura's Journey Lesson
God has the script for our unscripted lives.

I clung to my Bible that night and cried out to God. He showed me that the only script to follow in the "unscripted show" of dealing with cancer was to trust Him. My trust in God increased during this season. He was faithful to guide me, bring me peace, and give me wisdom for the decisions that I had to make. He walked by my side with every step I took. I'm so thankful that I didn't have to write the script for this show; God had it all written, and with His guidance, I walked through it.

The Day After

I didn't go to work the day after hearing the news that I had been diagnosed with cancer. I wrote my first entry in the secret Facebook Group that I set up. The group was called "Laura's Journey Series." The purpose of the group was to provide a forum for me to share my challenges and victories and to honor and glorify God through my journey.

I traveled a lot in my previous job and routinely shared about my travels on my personal Facebook page. Many of my friends and family commented how they so enjoyed going on the journeys with me. I wanted to take them on this new journey, and therefore I created the secret group. Here is my first post:

Post Written on October 10, 2012

Many of you have expressed how much you like to follow me on my journeys through my Facebook page.

I am embarking on a new journey in life. It is one that I didn't plan on, but I have no choice but to walk it out. I created a secret group to share because of the nature of the journey.

I received a diagnosis yesterday that will forever change my life – Grade 2 uterine cancer.

My journey will involve surgery and radiation treatments. I am waiting to see an oncologist. The appointment hasn't been scheduled yet. Despite all the emotions that roam through me, I do have God's peace that surpasses all understanding flowing through my soul. It is only by God's grace and strength that I will get through this.

Yes, I will be receiving physical treatments, but I also need God's treatments to carry me through. Therefore, I will be posting daily "God treatment" Scriptures that I'll meditate on throughout the day. Please feel free to meditate on these Scriptures too and post any thoughts or words of encouragement to this group. As I mentioned, this is a secret group ... so anything you post is only visible to the group members and no one else. Thank you for being a part of this journey with me. May we all grow in God and learn more about Him through it.

Several people posted comments within minutes after I uploaded my post and the comments kept pouring in throughout the day. By the end of the day, 22 people had left comments for me. Each time a person left a comment, my smartphone notified me that someone had left a comment. I immediately went and read comments as they were posted. The support was overwhelming, and I truly felt the love of God as I read the comments. Most times, the floodgate of tears opened again and again as I read. By the end of the day, my eyes were swollen because I had cried so much.

Learning Patience

Several days had passed, and I hadn't heard from the oncologist's office that my gynecologist recommended. My impatience busted at the seams. I couldn't take it any longer. I called the oncologist's office and spoke with the person at the front desk. She said that the doctor was evaluating my case to see if he would take me on as a patient. I wasn't doing the happy dance at this news. I'm thinking, "What! Why wouldn't he accept me as a patient?" I worked myself into a frenzy when I heard this; like I didn't have enough to worry about and now to heap on top of my worry pile, the fact that I might be rejected as a patient of the highly-acclaimed oncologist that my gynecologist recommended.

A few days passed when the person called me back to inform me the oncologist would see me and take me on as a new patient. Alleluia! My appointment was scheduled for one week out. Great! I had to wait longer before getting additional answers about my diagnosis.

I must admit it was worth the wait to meet my oncologist for the first time. He must have known I was an engineer because he started drawing pictures within 30 seconds of talking with me. The pictures assisted him in explaining the pathology report from the D&C procedure. His recommendation was to have a full hysterectomy. The surgery was scheduled for October 31, 2012. Another two weeks to wait. Sigh!

Surgery

God began to teach me about having patience in the storm. He reminded me that everything was done at His perfect time.

"For the vision is yet for an appointed time; But at the end it will speak, and it will not lie. Though it tarries, wait for it; Because it will surely come, it will not tarry." Habakkuk 2:3

God used this verse to teach me about His perfect timing.

Laura's Journey Lesson
God has an appointed time for everything that happens in our lives, and we must wait patiently for Him to move on our behalf.

I struggled with waiting for surgery and starting treatments. If it were up to me, I would have had surgery within an hour after hearing about the cancer diagnosis. You see, the cancer diagnosis gave me a sense that I had no control, and making decisions swiftly provided a way for me to regain my sense of control. Consequently, waiting was a challenge for me. Nevertheless, I wanted to experience the outcomes described in James 1:3-4:

"... knowing that the testing of your faith produces patience. But let patience have its perfect work, that you may be perfect and complete, lacking nothing."

Patience under this trial produced important effects in my soul that not only impacted my life, but the lives of others. My heart's desire was for God's will to be fulfilled in my life. Hence, I waited patiently for His perfect timing, knowing that I was being made perfect and complete through it all.

Psalm 46:10 was another verse that God used to show me to wait upon Him.:

He says, "Be still, and know that I am God; I will be exalted among the nations, I will be exalted in the earth!"

A co-worker gave me a coaster that referred to this Scripture shortly after being diagnosed with cancer. The coaster sits on my desk to remind me of His presence and that I can be still amidst the storms.

"Be still" meant I leave all matters with God, give no room to anxiety and have a calm, confident, and trusting state of mind because of God's divine presence and power in my life.

The day of surgery could have been a day where anxiety and worry consumed me. I fought these feelings by being focused on being still. This I knew: my God was watching over me and everything surrounding my surgery; my life was in His hands and there was no better place to be.

Surgery was over, and all went well. My doctor said that cancer had invaded 60%-70% of my uterine wall while the lymph nodes and everything else appeared to be normal; my ovaries and lymph nodes were removed too and were tested for cancer, which was standard procedure.

Considering the extent of cancer invasion into my uterus, my heart was full of joy that it was discovered before spreading to other parts of my body. God truly looked out for me, and I was so thankful for His presence in my life.

I spent one night in the hospital and went home the following day.

Laura's Journey Lesson
Meditating on God's Word instead of the "What if" questions brings peace and drives out worry and anxiousness.

Pathology Report

Practicing patience became a normal part of my recovery after surgery. I waited 10 days before receiving the pathology results from my doctor. I quickly learned to live my life to the fullest with the information that I had been given. I tried not to jump ahead and flood my mind with the "What if" questions like "What if the pathology report showed cancer had spread to the lymph nodes?" or "What if I need chemotherapy?" Thinking about these questions only filled me with anxiety and frustration. God taught me to meditate on His words in the Bible during this time.

Philippians 4:6-7 became one of my main go-to verses:

"Be anxious for nothing, but in everything by prayer and supplication, with thanksgiving, let your requests be made known to God; and the peace of God, which surpasses all understanding, will guard your hearts and minds through Christ Jesus."

I experienced a lot of anxiety after being diagnosed with cancer. Everyone told me that these were common feelings in situations like this. Nevertheless, I didn't like them. They depleted my energy and wore me down.

I was starved for God's peace that surpasses all understanding but was lost as to how to find it. I then realized that God's peace would come after I did two things: (1) bring my requests to God through prayer, and (2) give him thanks in everything – this meant giving Him thanks even as I dealt with cancer.

I must admit I didn't always do these things during my anxious times, but I learned to turn to prayer more quickly and give Him thanks for it all. In doing this,

I shifted my focus from the situation that caused me anxiety to focusing on God. As my mood lightened, peace replaced my anxiety. My prayer became, "Lord fill me with your peace that surpasses all understanding as I continue walking the journey out."

The day finally arrived! It was my follow-up appointment with my doctor.

My heart raced as the doctor walked in the room with the pathology report in his hand. My doctor said that the pathology report looked good and that all the lymph nodes and other organs removed didn't show signs of cancer. He said that cancer cells did show up in my blood, which was cause for concern. He said that I would need radiation treatment and he would consult with other specialists to see if chemotherapy would be needed. The doctor also shared there was a 96% cure rate with surgery and radiation treatment.

I left the doctor's office feeling like I had dodged a bullet and was thankful to God for the great news that I had just heard.

Treatment

I got to practice being patient again as I waited a week to meet with the radiation oncologist. My previous experiences after receiving the diagnosis taught me to live one day at a time without thinking ahead. Any time I caught myself thinking ahead, I took those thoughts captive to the obedience of Christ (2 Corinthians 10:5). I replaced those thoughts with the Scriptures that I shared in the previous pages.

Not only did I have to deal with the physical and emotional issues related to the diagnosis, but I also had to learn how to use God's Word to battle the thoughts in my mind. Little did I know that the battle in my mind was just the tip of the iceberg, considering what I went through in fighting fear later in my journey, which I describe in Chapter 7.

Meeting with the radiation oncologist was the first step of my treatment. The doctor reviewed the treatment plan with me, which consisted of four targeted radiation treatments.

I approached radiation treatment like it was a new adventure. The preparation time for the treatment was 2.5 hours followed by 6 minutes of radiation. I listened to Christian music during preparation and treatment. Worship music became my way to keep focused on God through it all. There were many times that God spoke to me through these worship times. One time He brought to my mind Hebrews 13:5:

"...For He Himself has said, 'I will never leave you nor forsake you."

God was with me as I underwent radiation treatment. The physical pain of treatment intensified with each treatment. This didn't matter. I rested in knowing that He was with me and prepared every detail and anointed the radiation technicians to do His work in my life. His presence got me through, and I was thankful.

I didn't experience many side effects from the radiation treatment because it was targeted to the specific area where the cancer was located. I went back to work before my radiation treatments started and continued working as I went through each one. Although the pain became unbearable during the treatment, I was so thankful that it quickly left when treatment was over.

My mom, friend, and I went out to dinner after my last treatment to celebrate. It was such a huge relief to have surgery and treatment behind me. I remember thinking that it was over and I would never have to undergo surgery and treatment ever again. Little did I know that cancer would come back a year later.

Chapter 3
Seeking God's Purpose

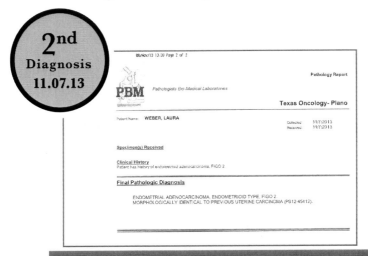

2nd
Diagnosis
11.07.13

Pathology Report

PBM Pathologists Bio-Medical Laboratories

Texas Oncology- Plano

Patient Name: WEBER, LAURA

Collected: 11/7/2013
Received: 11/7/2013

Specimen(s) Received

Clinical History
Patient has history of endometrioid adenocarcinoma, FIGO 2

Final Pathologic Diagnosis

ENDOMETRIAL ADENOCARCINOMA, ENDOMETRIOID TYPE, FIGO 2.
MORPHOLOGICALLY IDENTICAL TO PREVIOUS UTERINE CARCINOMA (PS12-45412).

Endometrial Adenocarcinoma - Identical to previous Uterine Carcinoma

Treatment:
Radiation 5 days/week for 5 weeks followed by
3 high-dose radiation treatments

Hearing the Words Again

After the radiation treatments were completed, I went
for CT scans and blood work every three months. For
the most part, I wasn't too concerned because the doctor
told me that I should never have to deal with having

the cancer return because the surgery and radiation treatment success rate was 96%. I lived like cancer was a thing of the past, and I would never have to deal with it again.

Shortly after celebrating my one-year anniversary post-surgery, I developed symptoms that possibly indicated a return of cancer. The symptoms developed over the weekend. Because of my concern, I called the on-call oncologist staff person. I left a message for them to call me back.

My mind raced a thousand miles a minute thinking that cancer had returned. I became unraveled waiting for the oncologist to call me back.

The phone rang about 45 minutes after I had left the message. I answered and shared with the oncologist what I was experiencing. I remember asking him, "Does this mean cancer has returned?" I wanted an answer right then and there. I needed to know to put my mind at ease. He said he didn't know, but recommended that I schedule an appointment with my regular oncologist the coming week. His answer didn't ease my mind.

First thing Monday morning, I called my oncologist and was in his office the next day. He examined me and assured me that the symptoms were related to scar tissue that developed from the surgery and the radiation treatments. He put me on a treatment protocol designed to reduce the scar tissue. When I returned after a month of treatment, he took a biopsy of the tissue as a precaution. Four days later the doctor called and told me the biopsy was positive for cancer.

Anger boiled up in my soul after I got off the phone. The anger wasn't directed at God or any one person, but rather, I was angry that I had to go through this again. The uncertainty of the future and the fact that cancer came back again to rule my life bothered me. Nevertheless, the Lord reminded me of Proverbs 3:5-6:

"Trust in the Lord with all your heart and lean not on our understanding; in all ways acknowledge Him and He will direct your paths."

This is all I could do – acknowledge God and look to Him for guidance.

I met with the oncologist two days after receiving the phone call. He shared that the tumor was about the size of a pencil eraser and felt confident that we caught it early enough. Radiation was the recommended treatment approach.

Treatment

I met with the radiation oncologist four days later to discuss the treatment approach. He said we needed to be aggressive because this wasn't a good situation. He told me that I would receive the maximum dosage of radiation to the pelvic area. Treatment would occur five days a week for five weeks, followed by three highly-targeted radiation treatments. He shared about the short- and long-term side effects that I might experience. He made it very clear that we needed to attack this with a vengeance and wanted to know that I was on board.

Did I have a choice? I mean, cancer returned and was growing in my body and would continue to grow without treatment. I also knew from my previous research that a recurrence for my type of cancer had a poor prognosis. I agreed to the treatment protocol in hopes that I would finally be healed.

The radiation oncologist also recommended I have a PET scan to see if cancer had spread to other areas of my body. I agreed, and a request for approval was submitted to my insurance company. The request was denied. The insurance company stated they don't cover costs for PET scans for my type of cancer.

I didn't need the added frustration of the insurance company. I was already dealing with a lot and to have this heaped on me was too unbearable. I decided to go ahead with the PET scan and pay out of pocket.

I completed the PET scan first thing in the morning, and the doctor's office said they would call me by the end of the day to let me know the results. It was approaching 4 p.m., and I hadn't heard from the doctor's office. Waiting for the news was like having a heavy weight on my back that was crushing me. I kept asking myself, "What will I do if cancer has spread throughout my body?" This was the first time that I had come face-to-face with the fact that death may be a real possibility for me. I didn't like thinking about it.

I couldn't wait any longer. I called the doctor's office and left a message for the doctor's nurse. My phone rang about 30 minutes later, and my caller ID indicated it was the doctor's office. With my heart racing, I answered the phone. It was the doctor's nurse. She said, "Laura, you do realize that I'm calling instead of the doctor because your PET scan shows that the cancer was localized to the area where the biopsy was taken." She continued, "If it had spread, you'd be talking with the doctor instead of me."

The weight I had felt instantly left me when the nurse shared this news with me. I felt it was a huge victory; I praised God and then went to dinner to celebrate.

Before starting radiation treatments, I received three pin-head sized tattoos. Yes, tattoos! I wanted to have fun with this. I posted on Facebook that I got three tattoos in honor of starting treatment. It was fun reading all the responses I received. A few days later, I shared the real reason why I got the tattoos: they were strategically placed to help the radiation techs properly align the radiation machine concentrating the radiation only to the area where the tumor was located.

My first radiation treatment occurred after Thanksgiving Day in 2013 and treatments continued until the first week in February 2014. Side effects were minimal with the biggest being fatigue.

I truly believe there was one reason why the radiation side effects were minimal in my case. As I began radiation treatments, my prayer was, "Lord, I place the blood of Jesus over my healthy cells, tissues, and organs. Allow the radiation to pass over them with no impact and destroy only the cancer cells." This prayer was based on the Scripture verse found in Exodus 12:23:

"For the Lord will pass through to strike the Egyptians; and when He sees the blood on the lintel and on the two doorposts, the Lord will pass over the door and not allow the destroyer to come into your houses to strike you."

This verse describes how God protected the Israelites during Passover. God instructed them to mark their door posts with the blood from the slaughtered spring lamb. The blood symbolizes the blood of Jesus, and God didn't allow the destroyer to come into their houses to strike them because they were protected by the blood.

God's Purpose

My faith remained strong despite the recent recurrence of cancer. During treatment, I read an article that listed several steps to deal with cancer. One of the steps was to define what it meant to be a cancer patient or survivor.

I decided to define what it meant to be diagnosed with cancer. My definition was that cancer gave me an opportunity to reflect the glory of the Lord in my life and become more like Him. I wasn't thankful for cancer, but I was thankful for the opportunity of the Lord to use it to reveal Him more to me and others. The following Scripture became my mission:

"But we Christians have no veil over our faces; we can be mirrors that brightly reflect the glory of the Lord. And as the Spirit of the Lord works within us, we become more and more like Him."
2 Corinthians 3:18 (TLB)

My prayer became that I would brightly reflect God's glory and become more like Him through it all. This decision was a turning point for me and created a tectonic shift in my attitude. I looked for opportunities to share the goodness of God with others.

Using Our God-Given Weapons to Overcome Battles

God led me to an in-depth study of David and Goliath. It all began on a Sunday night at my church's connect group meeting.

Focusing on the meetings shortly after receiving the news of my biopsy results was challenging. My mind was consumed with other thoughts about my circumstances. I wasn't paying attention to the current conversation when one comment about a previous discussion from the year before broke through my scattered thoughts like a blaring horn. I don't remember the exact words of the comment, but it had to do with remembering what God has brought you through when facing current situations in your life.

1 Samuel 17:37 came to mind.

"...The Lord, who delivered me from the paw of the lion and from the paw of the bear, He will deliver me from the hand of this Philistine."

I meditated on this verse all week after the meeting and reminded myself of how God not only brought me through cancer last year but how He delivered and healed me from so many "cancers of the soul." This current Philistine (cancer) will be just like one of them; God will also deliver me! It is not up to me to figure out how God will do it, but like David, I must walk in boldness and faith that God will deliver me. This became my resolve, and I purposed in my mind to walk through the journey with boldness and confidence in God's delivering power over my situation.

I continued my study of 1 Samuel 17:38-40 and 48-50:

"So Saul clothed David with his armor, and he put a bronze helmet on his head; he also clothed him with a coat of mail.

David fastened his sword to his armor and tried to walk, for he had not tested them. And David said to Saul, 'I cannot walk with these, for I have not tested them.' So David took them off.

Then he took his staff in his hand; and he chose for himself five smooth stones from the brook, and put them in a shepherd's bag, in a pouch which he had, and his sling was in his hand. And he drew near to the Philistine.

So it was, when the Philistine arose and came and drew near to meet David, that David hurried and ran toward the army to meet the Philistine.

Then David put his hand in his bag and took out a stone; and he slung it and struck the Philistine in his forehead, so that the stone sank into his forehead, and he fell on his face to the earth.

So David prevailed over the Philistine with a sling and a stone, and struck the Philistine and killed him. But there was no sword in the hand of David."

The story of David and Goliath was such a great story about one man's faith to overcome the impossible defeat of a giant in his life. This was the exact journey I was on: the journey of my faith to overcome what seemed to be an impossible battle with a giant called cancer. The battle ultimately belonged to the Lord, but just like David, I needed to arise, meet the battle head on, and use my God-given weapons to defeat the giant.

Laura's Journey Lesson
We must use our weapons that have worked in past battles to gain victory in our current battles.

The Scripture verse above describes David's selection of his weapons for battle. Saul initially tried to give his weapons to David. These weapons obviously didn't give David confidence, and they immobilized him (see verse 39). Confidence and mobility were two things David needed for the battle. David went back to the weapons with which he was familiar: the staff, five smooth stones, shepherd's bag, and sling. These weapons seemed insufficient for the giant, but David knew they worked for him in past battles, and he had confidence that they'd work in taking down Goliath.

Just like Saul, many people suggested various things to help me deal with cancer. And just like David, I had to choose my weapons that I was familiar with, gave me the confidence, and knew had worked for me in my past battles.

My weapons were:

- Daily Scripture reading - My faith increased as I read God's Word. (Romans 10:17)

- Prayer - Through prayer, strongholds were pulled down. (2 Corinthians 10:4)

- Worship – I shifted my focus from my circumstance to God's majesty and power. (Psalm 29:1-2)

- Temple of the Holy Spirit - My body was the temple of the Holy Spirit, and I had to be a good steward to strengthen it through proper nutrition and exercise. (1 Corinthians 6:19)

- Fellowship with other believers – I had support from friends and family to keep me encouraged. (Hebrews 10:24)

My weapons increased my trust in God. These weapons had worked for me in past battles, and I was confident that they'd do the same as I continued my journey. And just like David, I selected them based on comfort and familiarity. With God and my weapons, victory belonged to me!

1 Samuel 17: 40 was my next verse for study and meditation.

"Then he took his staff in his hand; and he chose for himself five smooth stones from the brook, and put them in a shepherd's bag, in a pouch which he had, and his sling was in his hand..."

This Scripture looks at the weapons David chose to defeat Goliath. My focus was on two of the weapons David chose: the staff and five smooth stones.

The first weapon referenced in the Scripture was David's staff. Remember, David was a shepherd, and all shepherds carried a rod and staff. Each served a different purpose. The rod was a club used to discipline the sheep and defend against predators attacking the sheep. The staff, with its hook shape on the top, was used to rescue sheep when they went astray or guide them back to the flock when wandering off. The rod and staff also symbolize God's discipline and power (rod) and guidance (staff) for our lives. It was interesting that David selected the staff (God's guidance) rather than the rod (God's power) to take into battle with him. Did his selection of the staff over the rod indicate that having

God's guidance was more important than having God's power? Did God's guidance lead David to select five smooth stones, which I later suggest represents God's divine grace?

I pondered and researched the reason why David selected five smooth stones. Why did he select five? Why was it important that they were smooth? The Bible doesn't provide any answers to these two questions, but I found numerous answers from commentaries and other sources.

There was a consensus among the commentaries that the stones needed to be smooth so they would fly perfectly through the air when he threw them from his sling. Smooth stones ensured David would have the accuracy needed to hit Goliath and kill him.

Laura's Journey Lesson
We need God's guidance, divine power, and grace when fighting giants in our lives. God's guidance gives us the battle plan for victory, while His divine power and grace sustains us through the battle.

I found many suggestions as to why David selected five stones. Two of the most common included:

David would need to defend himself against Goliath's four brothers after he killed Goliath. (However, the Bible only references one brother for Goliath, so this didn't seem plausible to me.)

Another theory relates to the significance of the number five in the Bible. Five is the number that symbolizes God's divine grace. The fact that David chose stones and a sling as the weapons to use against a much stronger opponent indicated that he was relying on God's grace – and not his strength – for victory. Although I don't know why David selected five stones, I tend to agree with this reasoning.

This Scripture verse showed me that I needed God's guidance, divine power, and grace when fighting giants in my life. I tended to believe that God's guidance needed to come first because it gave me the battle plan to follow as I fought my battle with cancer. God's divine power and grace would sustain me through the battle and lead me to victory if I continued following the guidance given by God.

Asking the Correct "What" Question

One Sunday in church, we sang the song titled "O the Blood." As I sang the song, my mind kept thinking about the sacrifice that Jesus went through and the pain and suffering He experienced because of His love for me. As the song continued, a question arose from my soul: "Laura, is what Jesus did on the cross sufficient for you to trust in God, walk in faith, and turn away from sin?"

Fear is one thing that I had struggled with over the past few months, especially as my treatment came to an end. The "What if" questions roamed through my mind. You know the ones: What if the radiation didn't kill all cancer? What if cancer comes back? What if...? There are many "What if" questions.

I realized Sunday that I was asking the wrong "what" question. Look back to the question that arose from my soul during the song: "Laura, is what Jesus did on the cross sufficient...?" This was the "what" question I needed to be asking. Was His pain and suffering sufficient for me to trust that God is my healer and not the radiation? Yes, He uses the radiation, but my ultimate healing comes from Him. I needed to walk in faith and believe that I was healed by the stripes of Jesus (Isaiah 53:5) and not doubt, for doubting is unbelief and unbelief is sin (Romans 14:23).

There were three ways for me to answer the question that arose from my soul during this song: no; yes, I don't walk by faith for my healing; or yes, I do walk in faith. The first two answers mock what Jesus did on the cross for me and lead to sin. The third answer is the only one that doesn't mock Jesus and embraces the fullness of all that Christ did for me on the cross.

I encourage you to ask yourself, "Is what Jesus did on the cross sufficient for you to trust in God, walk in faith, and turn away from sin?" I know you may not be dealing with cancer, but there may be other areas in your life in which you haven't fully trusted God, walked in faith, and turned away from sin. The cross can take care of these areas if you choose the third answer.

Chapter 4
Choose Life, Trust God

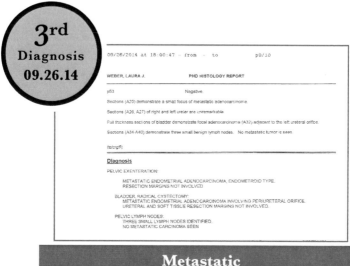

3rd
Diagnosis
09.26.14

WEBER, LAURA J.   PHD HISTOLOGY REPORT

p53   Negative.

Sections (A25) demonstrate a small focus of metastatic adenocarcinoma.

Sections (A26, A27) of right and left ureter are unremarkable.

Full thickness sections of bladder demonstrate focal adenocarcinoma (A32) adjacent to the left ureteral orifice.

Sections (A34-A40) demonstrate three small benign lymph nodes.   No metastatic tumor is seen.

(tp/crg/fl)

Diagnosis

PELVIC EXENTERATION:

    METASTATIC ENDOMETRIAL ADENOCARCINOMA, ENDOMETROID TYPE.
    RESECTION MARGINS NOT INVOLVED

BLADDER, RADICAL CYSTECTOMY:
    METASTATIC ENDOMETRIAL ADENOCARCINOMA INVOLVING PERIURETERAL ORIFICE.
    URETERAL AND SOFT TISSUE RESECTION MARGINS NOT INVOLVED.

PELVIC LYMPH NODES:
    THREE SMALL LYMPH NODES IDENTIFIED.
    NO METASTATIC CARCINOMA SEEN

Metastatic Endometrial Adenocarcinoma

Treatment:
Surgery

I entered a new phase of my journey. It was the phase after treatment. This phase involved follow up CT scans and blood work every three months with my oncologist. Although my mind liked to think about these future checkups and worry about the outcomes, I clung to Matthew 6:34:

"Therefore do not worry about tomorrow, for tomorrow will worry about its own things. Sufficient for the day is its own trouble."

I resolved not to worry, to focus on living in the present, and enjoy my life one day at a time.

This was challenging when one of my CT scans showed abnormal results. As a precaution, my doctor ordered a PET scan. I was thankful to hear that the PET scan was negative for cancer. But that changed a month later.

I saw my oncologist for what I thought were issues with scar tissue related to the radiation treatments. During the exam, my doctor felt something that concerned him. I had a biopsy four days later. He said that they would only call if the results were positive for cancer.

I had the biopsy on a Tuesday. My phone rang Thursday, and the call was from the doctor's office. My heart sank as I answered. The nurse said that they needed to see me as soon as possible. I asked her, "Does this mean it is bad news?" All she said was, "I'm sorry, Ms. Weber," followed by, "Can you come in this afternoon?" I called a friend to go with me, and packed up my things and left my office. As I drove to my friend's house, all I thought was that the words "you have cancer" were beginning to sound like a broken record to me. My mind raced forward to thinking about treatment options, which I knew would be limited because I had already received the maximum dosage of radiation to the area where cancer came back.

As my friend and I met with the doctor, he explained that the tumor was localized and small, which was a good thing. He explained that treatment options were limited because of the amount of radiation that I had already received in the area. He recommended a radical surgery. He said that the surgery had a 25% cure rate. My initial thought was, "Only 25%? That doesn't sound very good!" However, I asked him, "You must think I'm in that 25% group because you wouldn't recommend the surgery if I weren't?" He responded, "Yes," which made me feel a little better. My doctor also recommended that I get a second opinion at MD Anderson, the number one cancer center in the United States.

I kept thinking about how I had asked God at the beginning of my journey not to let me arrive at the place where I was now. It was a spot where only radical surgery was the curative option. I knew much about the surgery he recommended because of my research at the beginning of my journey. I always said that I wouldn't have the surgery if I got to the place where I needed it. Now I was in that place, and I had to decide what I was going to do.

I slept with my Bible the first night after finding out about that cancer recurrence. When I woke up, I read Psalm 36:7-9:

"How precious is Your lovingkindness, O God! Therefore, the children of men put their trust under the shadow of Your wings. They are abundantly satisfied with the fullness of Your house, and You give them drink from the river of Your pleasures. For with You is the fountain of life; In Your light, we see light."

I needed God's lovingkindness more than ever in my life and put my trust under the shadow of His wings. I needed to be in the fullness of His house and drink from His river of pleasures. Oh, how could I reach that place of fully trusting Him when the raging storm was swirling around me? God used my trip to MD Anderson to show me that He was faithful and was with me every step of the way.

Trip to MD Anderson

My prayer as I went to MD Anderson was that God would show me His will for treatment. I needed His guidance more than ever, and I wanted it to be very clear to me. God powerfully answered my prayer.

I met a guy from the RV park where we were staying during our shuttle ride to my appointment at MD Anderson. This guy seemed to have a joy deep inside him that was contagious. He began to ask me about my situation and why I was there. I told him, and then he shared with me that his cancer was terminal. In the end, he gave me an F.R.O.G. coin that forever changed my life. The coin had a picture of a frog on one side and the Scripture reference to Isaiah 26:4:

"Trust in the Lord forever, for in YAH, the Lord, is everlasting strength."

The side with the picture of the frog had these large printed words: Fully Rely on God (F.R.O.G.)

When I arrived at the building for my appointment, I had time to sit and read my morning devotional titled, "Walk with Me Along the Paths of Trust." And yes, Isaiah 26:4 was presented again to me during my

devotional. God was sending me a message to trust in Him no matter what the outcome would be.

The doctors at MD Anderson agreed with my doctor in Dallas that surgery was the best option and presented the best opportunity for curing me of cancer. The doctors also told me that my surgeon in Dallas was the best and they would select him to do the surgery if they were in my shoes. Consequently, I returned home and I visited my surgeon in Dallas to discuss surgery and begin the scheduling process.

God answered my prayer that there would be no doubt as to the decision I would need to make. The doctors at MD Anderson were very clear about this being the only option for me and that my doctor in the Dallas area was the most experienced and qualified. I thank the Lord for the clarity and showing me the way.

Overall, I had much peace with my decision. I continued trusting the Lord with every aspect of my life. I didn't understand why I had to walk on this path, but that was okay. God was in control, I was in His hands, and I didn't want to be anywhere else.

Keeping my focus on God and believing that He had a purpose for me going through the surgery was key for me reaching a place of fully trusting Him. Matthew 14:22-32 describes the story of Peter walking on water during a raging storm. He got out of the boat and began walking on water because he wanted to go to Jesus. This was truly a miracle, but as soon as he took his eyes off Jesus and focused on the storm, he began to sink. I too wanted to go to Jesus, and I purposed in my heart and mind to keep Jesus the center of my attention as I continued preparing for a surgery that would drastically change my life.

Surgery

Pelvic exenteration was the recommended surgery to save my life. It was a radical procedure designed to remove my pelvic organs that either had cancer or had the potential to develop cancer after surgery. I knew there would be the possibility that the surgeon would need to remove my colon, bladder, and the affected area where the cancer was located. If the colon and bladder were removed, then I would live the rest of my life with a colostomy and urostomy. The surgeon told me that the surgery could take 8-12 hours, but that he usually completes it in 4-5 hours. He also told me that there was a long recovery time. I'd be in the hospital at least seven days after surgery and would need to be off work for six months. He also had me see a plastic surgeon because I would need reconstructive surgery after my main surgeon was done with his part.

When this surgery option was first presented to me, I said I would never do it because I didn't want to spend the rest of my life wearing two external bags to collect my poop and urine. Nevertheless, God slowly began to work in my heart to bring me to a place of fully trusting Him with this surgical procedure.

"Choose life. Trust in the Lord."

These were the words from God as I researched the surgical procedure and consulted with my doctors. My trust in the Lord increased as the day of surgery approached, and God gave me the confidence that everything would turn out for my own good. My life was in His hands, and there was no other place that I wanted to be. The Lord was with me in a very powerful

way, and my love for Him continued to grow as I
continued my journey.

I wrote in my journal the night before surgery:

"Twas the night before surgery
No worry or anxiety can be found
God's peace overfills my soul
I'm thankful for God's presence in my life
His love for me is amazing
Good night to all."

I arose the next morning and arrived at the hospital
around 6 a.m. I had so much peace that morning –
I truly experienced the peace that surpasses all
understanding as it is written in Philippians 4:7. The
verse states that I'm to let my requests be made known
to God through prayer and supplication. I truly believe I
had so much peace because I laid down my life and told
God that I was His willing servant for His will in my
life. I didn't understand why cancer kept coming back or
why I had to go through this surgery, but it didn't matter
because I trusted God to bring me through.

My primary surgeon came to the waiting area about
three hours into the surgery. He shared with my family
and friends that surgery went well and that the cancer

was contained in one area. He said that the second surgeon was doing the reconstructive surgery now and that I should be out in about 1 ½ hours.

One of my prayers was that I would only need my bladder removed and not my colon. Somehow, I knew that I could live with a urostomy, but not a colostomy.

I slowly woke up in the recovery room. My first thought was, "Did I have two bags or one bag?" My mom and I agreed that when they allowed her to come back to the waiting area, she would raise two fingers for two bags or one finger for one bag. I was in a lot of pain, and my blood pressure was very low. I was so cold that I felt I was lying naked in the Arctic. I could hear the nurses talking about me having an ileostomy. I didn't know that word because my doctor never talked about it. They finally let my mom visit me. I remember her smile as she peeked her head around the curtain. She had one finger up and mouthed the word urostomy to me. I began to cry with joy and gave thanks to the Lord for answering my prayer.

Recovery

I was in the recovery area for about 2-3 hours before being placed in a room. My memory of the first 12 hours after surgery was foggy because of all the pain medicine. The only thing I remember was being extremely cold. I have never felt cold like I did then. They wrapped me up in warm blankets from head to toe and kept changing them out to keep me warm.

The first day after surgery was challenging. My oncologist visited me in the morning. He shared with me how pleased he was with the surgery and ensured me that the outcomes were better than expected. He asked me about getting up and walking throughout the day. I shared with him that I felt dizzy and would prefer to wait for a day. He said that was fine.

The respiratory therapist was the next person to visit me. She gave me an incentive spirometer. If you've ever been through surgery, you've probably had to use one of these too. It is an apparatus where you blow in a tube to lift a ball up to a certain amount on the measuring scale. The respiratory therapist wanted me to blow in the tube and raise the ball to three quarters of the measuring scale. I tried my best, but I could only get up to about 25%. The pain in my abdomen area was too intense, and I couldn't take in deep breaths. The respiratory therapist didn't seem to care about this. She began to tell me about the consequences of not able to do these exercises and the potential of pneumonia and possible dying from this condition. She became unraveled when I told her I wouldn't be getting up during the day because of my dizziness.

When the respiratory therapist left, I lost it and began crying. My friend asked what was wrong with me, but I couldn't tell her because I didn't know. I guess all my emotions busted out of me at once. I continued crying throughout the day and didn't know why.

My friend knew how much worship music ministered to me. She took my phone and turned my worship music on and let it play throughout the day and night until the next morning. Through my friend, God knew exactly what I needed to feel His presence and comfort. Although I was emotional for the rest of the day, the music soothed my weary soul and brought much comfort and peace.

Day 2 in the hospital went much better than the first. The intensity of my pain was subsiding, and I was gradually raising that little ball in the spirometer. I also got up for the first time and walked around the hall. The physical therapist helped me get out of bed. When I first stood up, I felt like all my pelvic organs were readjusting to their new space. After all, a few organs were missing, and my remaining ones had new places they could explore.

I was released from the hospital seven days after surgery just as my surgeon said. It was so nice to get outside of the hospital. It was about a 45-minute ride home from the hospital. I began crying as we left the hospital. I became overwhelmed with gratitude to God because of the outcomes of the surgery, which were better than expected. The cancer was contained in one area; the pathology report showed that no cancer was present in the lymph nodes or the bladder, which was removed as a precautionary measure. I didn't have my colon removed because the location of the primary tumor was far enough away from the colon.

Recovery was a long process as my doctor had advised. Because of the reconstructive surgery, I could only sit for a few minutes at a time. This meant that I spent most days either standing, lying down, or sitting reclined in a chair. I also had to be trained how to take care of my urostomy and change my appliance. Yes, the whole bag system for the urostomy was called an appliance. I had a health care nurse visit the house three times a week during the first few weeks of being home.

I purposed in my mind to maintain a positive attitude and do what I could physically, including taking short walks. I always needed a nap after my short walks. I finally worked up to swimming laps in the pool. My strength kept increasing with each passing day. It was a good thing, because I was diagnosed for the fourth time five months after my surgery.

Chapter 5

God is in Control

1/18/2015 08:18 FAX   TEXAS RADIOLOGY ASSOCIAT   ☑001/002

IMAGING REPORT
TEXAS RADIOLOGY ASSOCIATES, LLP

Patient: Name: Laura Weber

Order:
    Date: 3/18/2015 8:12 AM
    Procedure: PET/CT

    PLANO WEST CANCER CENTER
    TEXAS RADIOLOGY ASSOCIATES, LLP
    CONSULTING RADIOLOGISTS

PATIENT NAME: Laura Weber

EXAM: PET/CT from 3/18/2015 8:45 AM

HISTORY: Uterine cancer

TECHNIQUE: Approximately 1 hour after the injection of 14.2 mCi of F-18 FDG, whole body PET/CT was performed from the skull base to the mid thighs. The patient's blood glucose level was 83 mg/dl. CT was performed primarily for attenuation correction and anatomic localization. Images were reviewed on an independent GE workstation.

COMPARISON: PET/CT from June 30, 2014. CT from February 26, 2015

Impression:

2 metastatic left abdominal retroperitoneal lymph nodes with maximum SUV of 5.7.

Endometrial Carcinoma - Two metastatic left abdominal retroperitoneal lymph nodes

Treatment:

Radiation treatment, 5 days/week for 5 weeks; hormonal treatment
1 pill/day forever

You Have Cancer

As I recovered from the surgery, my gratitude to God grew day-by-day.

My first CT scan occurred five months after my pelvic exenteration surgery. I was feeling confident that good results were in store for me. However, this was not the case.

The scan showed that one of my lymph nodes was enlarged from my previous scan before my last surgery. Because of my history, this was concerning to my oncologist. As a precaution, the doctor ordered a PET scan, which I went through a few days later.

As I sat waiting for the oncologist to enter with the results from the PET scan, I remained hopeful that it showed no cancer. However, when I saw the look on my doctor's face, I knew the results were not good. The PET scan showed not one, but two of my lymph nodes were cancerous. My doctor said that this was highly unusual because none of my removed lymph nodes from the previous two surgeries were cancerous. He said that my cancer wasn't behaving like normal.

My heart sank when he said cancer had returned. This was the fourth time in 2 ½ years that I had heard these words. My steadfast trust in God didn't waiver. I purposed in my heart to keep pursuing and trusting God as my journey continued.

After I returned home from the doctor's office, I wrote the following letter to God in my journal:

"There were so many emotions that stirred in me today. From anxiousness to sadness and now Your peace that surpasses all understanding. I'm also excited; strange that I should feel the excitement in one of my darkest circumstances in life. Being diagnosed with cancer for the fourth time in 2 ½ years isn't something to be excited about. Nevertheless, I know deep down in my heart that You are in control, God, and You will not fail me. I also know that I have another opportunity to deepen my relationship with You and learn what it means to live by Your grace to continue the journey. I fully believe and expect that one day I will be healed. Until that day, I will continue to trust in You and live my life in a manner that honors and glorifies You. I love You, Lord, and I'm so glad You are carrying me on this journey." (March 20, 2015)

Many people asked me how I had such a positive outlook and unwavering faith in my darkest moments. I saw that I had two choices:

- Turn away from God and have nothing to do with Him ever again

- Run toward Him, fully embrace Him, and trust that His word is true and would work in my life

I knew the first choice would surely lead to frustration, more anxiety, and, ultimately, death. The second choice gave me hope that one day I would be totally healed from cancer, not to mention the experience of God's comfort and peace. To me, the choice was easy. How about you? I hope that you'd choose the second option in your darkest moments.

Laura's Journey Lesson
We have two choices when faced with trials. We can either run away from God or toward Him. Running away leads to frustration and death. Running toward Him gives us hope, comfort, and peace.

The lymph nodes were located just above my belly button, which was out of the treated area from my previous radiation treatments. This meant that I could receive radiation to the lymph nodes, and this was the primary recommended treatment option. My oncologist also suggested that I go on hormone therapy to block any cancer cells feeding on estrogen. For my type of cancer, estrogen acts like the energizer bunny to the cancer cells, causing them to grow. The hormone therapy would block the cancer cells from having access to the estrogen.

Treatment

I met with the radiologist oncologist the following week to discuss the radiation treatment. He said that we needed to be aggressive and that I'd be receiving the maximum dosage allowed. He said, "The horse is out of the barn now, and we need to stop it." His phrasing accurately described the situation – cancer was in my lymph system now and could spread to anywhere in my body. He did feel that radiation would kill the existing cancer and stop its spread throughout my body.

The treatment schedule was similar to my previous radiation treatments: five days a week for five weeks, for a total of 25 treatments. I also got three more tattoos, which allowed the techs to properly line up the radiation machine so that only the lymph nodes would get treated.

I tolerated this round of radiation much better than the first time. I had less fatigue, and I kept working. I attributed this to the fact that I made significant changes to my diet after my surgery. I eliminated sugar and mainly ate organic food. In a sense, I was giving my body the highest-octane fuel available. I also added a doctor to my team who took an integrative treatment approach. This meant she used both traditional and non-traditional approaches to treating cancer patients. I began to get monthly acupuncture treatments that were designed to super charge my immune system.

Continuing to Live Life to the Fullest

I came to understand the Scripture in James 4:14:

"Whereas you do not know what will happen tomorrow. For what is your life? It is even a vapor that appears for a little time and then vanishes away."

As my journey continued, I learned to live life like it was a vapor, here today and gone tomorrow. This meant that I took every opportunity to live my life to the fullest, enjoy it, and not get stressed over the small stuff. God opened many doors for me to do just this.

Fashion Show

A friend of mine shared information about Cuisine for Healing (CFH) as I was recovering from my second surgery. CFH is an organization that envisions a world where cancer and other related illnesses are prevented, treated, and eliminated through the power of healthy food. I began eating their meals after my surgery and have been eating them ever since. I also began volunteering with CFH, and, through this experience, I learned about their Survivors in Style (SIS) fashion show.

CFH invited me to participate as a model for their SIS fashion show while I was in treatment. I didn't immediately accept, but after praying about it, I decided to accept the invitation. I'm so glad I did. It was one of the best experiences I had during treatment.

May 7, 2015 was the evening where I joined 18 other cancer survivors and shared my story of triumph and hope with 450 people.

I participated in many preparatory steps before my debut as a model: attending a reception for the models, pre-recording my story in a professional recording studio, and selecting my outfit and getting fitted.

I arrived at the venue around 3 p.m. and was treated like a queen. Hair stylists and makeup artists transformed me into a beauty empress. After getting dressed, the other models and I practiced walking the runway and posed for photos.

I walked the runway once by myself and then with the whole group of models at the end of the show. It was truly a special evening for me. I found such inspiration from the other models, and listening to their stories brought me hope and encouragement as I continued my radiation treatment.

Running

There was a free fitness program for cancer patients and survivors at one of the cancer centers where I received treatment. Because I'm a fitness nut, I decided to meet with a trainer. She told me that my chances of recurrence could be reduced by 40% for my type of cancer by working out in my target heart zone for 150 minutes per week. After being diagnosed four times, I would do anything to reduce my recurrences. Running was the only activity that could get me to my target heart rate and sustain it. I became a runner, and I was quite shocked at how much I enjoyed it.

I ran my first 5K race on Thanksgiving Day in 2015. This was truly a miracle, considering that a year earlier, all I could do was walk 100 feet, let alone run. I wasn't even thinking about running then; all I wanted to do was walk without exhaustion consuming me.

I was so excited when I crossed the finish line! I felt like I had accomplished the impossible by God's grace. This race was a milestone in my journey and one that I'll never forget.

Running not only keeps me physically fit, but it also allows me to grow closer to God. I listen to worship music every time I run. There are many times God speaks profound words to me while running. Sometimes, I stop running because I get overwhelmed by His presence.

No Better Place

Although the news about my lymph nodes initially devastated and crippled me, I resolved in my heart to keep standing on God's Word and fight this disease that has been trying to destroy me. God was in control, and my life was in His hands; there was no better place for me to be. My faith remained strong, and I trusted God through it all. I lived my life one day at a time and to the fullest. I encourage you to do the same because you never know when you'll encounter a circumstance that changes your life forever.

Chapter 6
God Heals

IMAGING REPORT
TEXAS RADIOLOGY ASSOCIATES, LLP

Patient: Name: Laura Weber

Order:
Date: 4/25/2017 10:17 AM
Procedure: PET/CT

PLANO WEST CANCER CENTER
TEXAS RADIOLOGY ASSOCIATES, LLP
CONSULTING RADIOLOGISTS

PATIENT NAME: Laura Weber

EXAM: PET/CT from 4/25/2017 10:17 AM

HISTORY: Uterine cancer. Restaging.

TECHNIQUE: Approximately 1 hour after the injection of 12.3 mCi of F-18 FDG, whole body PET/CT was performed from the skull base to the mid thighs. The patient's blood glucose level was 88 mg/dl. CT was performed primarily for attenuation correction and anatomic localization. Images were reviewed on an independent workstation. ALARA principles followed.

COMPARISON: PET/CT from 3/18/2015. CT from 1/23/2017

FINDINGS:

Further increase in the metastatic left periaortic lymph node now measuring 2.1 cm with a maximum SUV of 18.6. On the prior CT this measured 1.4 cm. No other metabolically active lymph node is identified. There is no FDG evidence for osseous or hepatic metastatic disease. There is no metabolically active lung parenchymal abnormality. There is no FDG evidence for omental, peritoneal, or mesenteric metastatic disease.

Impression:

Enlarging highly metabolically active metastatic left periaortic lymph node.
Maximum SUV is 18.6.

Endometrial Carcinoma - Enlarging highly metabolically active metastatic left periaortic lymph node

---

Treatment:
None.
Doctor stopped hormonal treatment.

Shattered Confidence

All was going well for me, and I was feeling confident
that the cancer was behind me. My doctor told me
that I wouldn't need any more CT scans if my scan
in January 2017 was clear. What a joyous thought! No
more CT scans.

When the doctor walked into the room, the first
words out of his mouth were, "Your tumor markers
are elevated." As he passed me to sit down, I thought,
"Okay, no big deal." Then he shared with me that one
of the treated lymph nodes had increased in size. I
couldn't believe what I was hearing. He explained that
this was cause for concern because of my history. His
advice was to wait three months and do a PET scan to
see how things looked at that time. He also said it is very
uncommon for a recurrence of cancer so late after my
treatment and that the size of the lymph node is well
within normal range.

The excitement and confidence I felt when I walked
into the appointment had left me. My heart ached at
the thought that cancer had returned. Although the
doctor didn't say it had returned, I knew deep down
inside that this was probably the case. I also knew
that my treatment options would be limited because I

had already received the maximum radiation dosage to the lymph node. I remember thinking, "God, why God is this happening again?" I felt so bewildered and confused. When I got to my car, I sat in the seat and cried, hoping that my tears would somehow take away all the anguish that consumed me.

I pulled myself together, turned the ignition on, and started the drive home. I listened to worship music all the way home in hopes that the songs would help me make sense of the news I had just received. I kept telling myself, "Just live with the knowledge you know and don't try to make it into something that it's not." The knowledge was that the tumor markers were elevated and the lymph node had increased in size. That is all I knew; it hadn't been defined as cancer yet.

I reminded myself that I was most grateful for my journey through cancer and that this recent news showed me that the journey wasn't over yet. I stopped questioning God as to why this was happening again and clung to Romans 8:28 – that all things work together for my good. All meant everything, even these recent results from the CT scan and blood work.

Crossing Bridges

"Don't cross a bridge until it's time to cross." This was a phrase that one of my friends said to me throughout my journey.

I stood at the end of a bridge where there were no answers – only uncertainty and questions. It was a prime place for the devil to torment me with fear and anxiety. I decided that I wasn't going stay at this end, but rather, be proactive in getting ready for the arrival at the other end where I might hear that I have cancer for the fifth time. I knew deep in my heart that I needed to prepare myself for the worst news. Consequently, I embarked on an in-depth study of faith because I knew that my faith in Jesus needed to be rock solid for the news that I might hear in April.

Strengthen My Spiritual Muscles

My in-depth study of faith for three months helped to strengthen my spiritual muscles so that I could stand strong regardless of what news I would hear in April. As I sought God, He led me through my "spiritual workouts" which strengthened my faith.

The *Bible Faith Study Course* (Hagin, 1991) was the first book that I pulled from my bookcase because it provided a concentrated study about faith.

I'd come home from work and spend 30-45 minutes every night studying the faith principals presented in the book. I took my time with each chapter. I read them out loud and took notes in my journal to make sure that I wasn't missing anything.

The first principal I learned was that four things were required for healing:

- Hearing the Word of God
- Having faith to be healed
- Action
- Prayer of faith to change things

I completely understood the first item. Romans 10:17 presents the requirement for having faith:

"So then faith comes by hearing, and hearing by the word of God."

Number 2 was a challenge. How do I get the faith to be healed? Part of getting this kind of faith was to constantly read the Word of God and accept the truth of the Word of God without questioning and doubting the Word. I purposed in my mind and heart that the Word of God was the truth and that I wasn't going to question it.

I also learned the formula of faith that pleases God:

Faith that Pleases God = Have God's Word for what I desire + Believe God's Word + Don't consider the circumstances + Give praise to God for the answer

I love formulas because of my engineering background. This faith formula provided the roadmap that I needed to continue my preparation for arrival at the other end of the bridge.

I defined each part of the equation as:

- Have God's Word for what I desire
- My heart's desire was to be set free from cancer and never deal with it again. I immersed myself in God's Word as it related to healing.

Believe God's Word

I purposed in my heart to be like a little child that didn't question God's Word. I'd tell myself, "I know God's Word is true and it works! The stripes of Jesus healed me!" I believe what the Bible says, not what I see, hear, or feel.

Don't consider the circumstances

I didn't allow myself to dwell on the recent results. I kept my focus on God and His will for my life.

Give praise to God for the answer

I thanked God every day for my healing and setting me free from cancer.

In addition to studying Hagin's book, I began reading a book titled *Healed of Cancer* (Osteen, 2003), written by Dodie Osteen, the mother of Joel Osteen. She was diagnosed with metastatic cancer of the liver and only given a few weeks to live with or without treatment. She went home without receiving any treatment. This was in 1981, and she is alive today and free from cancer.

I met Dodie Osteen a few months before hearing the news about my CT scan while she was ministering at my church. As I sat and listened to her testimony of how God healed her of cancer without receiving any treatment, I thought of how thankful I was to be alive and well today and that I shouldn't have to deal with cancer ever again. I stood in line for hours waiting for Dodie to pray with me. It was a powerful time of personal prayer time, and I received a copy of her book.

I skimmed over her book when I first received it and placed it with all my other books in my bookcase. Little did I know then how instrumental her testimony and book would be in impacting my faith in healing.

A few main points from Dodie's book that captivated me:

- She acted as though she had already received her healing despite the pain and weakness she felt in her body.

- She studied healing Scriptures every day, saying "the Word of God saved her life."

I adopted Dodie's approach as I waited to have my PET scan. I began to read daily the healing Scripture references that were in Chapter 2 of her book. Additionally, I created my Scripture references and posted them all over my apartment. I developed a healing notes page with various Scriptures and faith principles that I could access from my phone at any time. I recited Psalm 118:17 every morning before I got out of bed.

"I shall not die, but live, and declare the works of the Lord."

I carried Dodie's book with me all the time and placed it on my desk at work. I read the book several times during the workday to remind myself of God's faithfulness to heal her and that He would heal me, too. Even after receiving my miracle, I still place her book on my desk and look through it several times a day. It now serves as a reminder to me about God's goodness and faithfulness to me.

Goliath Returns

On the Monday before I received the PET scan results, God reminded me of my study of David and Goliath in 2013. God had me zero in on the biblical significance of the number 5 and why David selected five stones to defeat Goliath. My conclusion was because David needed God's grace to defeat Goliath.

I didn't particularly like the fact that God reminded me of this study because of the significance of 5 as it related to the PET scan results. A positive PET scan result would mean that it would be the fifth diagnosis for me.

Deep down, I knew God was preparing me for the news, but oh, how I wanted the outcome to be different.

It was the night before I would receive the PET scan results. I had a range of emotions and thoughts roaming through me. I kept hoping for good results, but I lacked confidence that I would receive good news. All the medical evidence to date suggested the cancer was back. This, coupled with the study that God reminded me about on Monday night, gave me little hope that it was going to be good news. I tried focusing on God and not my circumstances, but it was challenging considering everything I was feeling. I was like a ship being tossed about a stormy sea. "Jesus! Please come and calm the storm on the inside of me," I whispered to Him.

As I continued seeking God, I thought about Jesus and the time He prayed three times in the Garden of Gethsemane (Matthew 26:39-44). I truly came to know what Jesus may have felt the night in Gethsemane. After all, He was human just as I am. What did He do? He prayed, "Father, please let this cup pass from me, yet not my will, but Your will be done."

Here is what I wrote in my journal that night:

*Oh, God, please let this cup of cancer pass me, but not my will,
but Your will be done. I know it is not Your will for me to have
cancer again, but I live in a fallen world where sicknesses exist.
If I trust you, Lord, then the results I get tomorrow won't matter.
Is this true, Lord? If the doctor tells me the cancer is back, what
does that mean? What does that do to my trust in You? You didn't
answer Jesus' prayer in the garden because You had a greater
purpose for Him through all the suffering — He suffered, then rose,
and was glorified. Is this what it would mean if the doctor tells
me the cancer is back — through my suffering You will be glorified?
This would require me to surrender my will to Yours — an act of
obedience just like Jesus. Am I willing to surrender my will in
this situation? I feel like I don't have a choice, but of course, I do
because You don't interfere with my will. My conclusion is that my
trust or belief in God will not change with a positive PET scan
result, it would only strengthen it.*

The next day I walked into the doctor's office hoping
for good news, but I knew deep down that I would hear
the words "you have cancer" again. I developed a list
of questions to ask the doctor if this was the case. I told
my friend who went with me that she was going to be
my secretary, and I asked her to write down the doctor's
answers to my questions.

I knew as soon as I saw the doctor that it wasn't good news. The PET scan showed that the lymph node was larger than the last scan, showing a clear indication of cancer. My tumor marker numbers had tripled from the previous value.

I pulled the list of questions from my bag, gave it to my friend, and began asking the doctor one by one. Treatment options were limited, and none of them were curative. The options included doing nothing, having surgery, and undergoing chemotherapy or a different hormone therapy. Surgery would be complicated and could be life threatening. Chemotherapy only had 25%-30% chance of working and would extend my life by 1-2 years. A different hormone therapy was even less likely to help than chemotherapy. My doctor suggested chemotherapy.

Tears flowed out of me as my friend and I walked out of the doctor's office. She put her arm around me as we walked out of the building and I said, "God must be up to something." I truly believed that He was. I had no idea what, but I just knew He was up to something.

Living a Victorious Life

Many people asked me how my faith remained strong during these darkest moments of battling cancer. As a young believer, I read a book titled *Victory Over Darkness* (Anderson, 2000). This book presents the truth of the Gospel – that we are free in Christ.

Neil presented the idea that if we believed what we felt instead of believing the truth, our lives would be inconsistent with what we felt instead of the truth. Scripture is truth and, I decided that I would study God's word, believe it, and live my life in the victory that Jesus won for me on the cross. I wasn't going to let my feelings or circumstances dictate my future. My faith grew day by day. I acted on my faith and continued to act until I was set free.

I genuinely believe that my search for truth in those early days planted deep roots in my soul for me to tap into as I battled cancer. My faith remained strong because of my initial sowing of God's word into my soul and my decision to always live a victorious life no matter what I faced.

Living a victorious life meant that I wasn't going to allow cancer to dictate my activities after getting the devastating news for the fifth time.

It was lunch time when we left the doctor's office, and we were hungry. Consequently, my friend and I went and ate lunch. After we returned to her home, I went running. I always listened to worship music during my runs, and on this day, I stopped in the middle of the run and sat on a bench near a pond with a fountain. I began to worship and praise God during this moment. Despite my feelings of anguish, God wrapped me in His grace and peace like only He could do. It was truly a moment of God showing and sealing His love for me deep in my soul.

Later that night, a few elders from my church joined my friends and me for a time of prayer. It was truly a special time in the Lord's presence that brought me much strength to face what was ahead of me.

Fifth Sunday

The Sunday after receiving the news of my fifth diagnosis was the fifth Sunday of the month. This was significant because it was Worship Sunday at my church. This meant there would be water baptisms and an extended time of worship. Before the service began, I received a text from my pastor's wife asking me to come to the front of the church so she could pray with me. She and other elders' wives anointed me with oil and prayed healing prayers over me. In my brokenness, I felt the Lord touch me, and I truly believed that God healed me during the prayer time.

I went back to my seat and waited for worship to begin, and when it did, I immediately walked to the altar. A few friends and elders joined me. I worshiped the Lord and cried the whole time. At one point, the worship leader looked down at me and asked what I was believing for. One of the elders said healing from recurrent cancer. The worship leader began to proclaim healing during worship. God met me in the river of my tears and brokenness and ministered His love to me. I felt such comfort and peace as worship continued.

Battle Plan

I was in the fight for my life now, and I needed God's battle plan to defeat the Goliath cancer once and for all. None of the traditional treatment options presented were curative. This meant that I needed a miracle to be victorious. I began to seek God's direction and guidance.

Amazingly, God gave me five components to my battle plan. Notice the significance of five again – God's grace.

1. David and Goliath

God kept taking me back to the story of David and Goliath. I read it every day to see what additional nuggets I could glean from the story. I learned two lessons from David: I must be determined and not lose heart; and I needed to speak confidently, have unwavering faith, and run toward my Goliath called cancer.

Goliath Threatens (1 Samuel 17:8-10)

Verbally threatening the Israelites was the first thing that Goliath did. He did it in such a manner that it frightened the Israelites and gave them no hope for winning.

The Goliath called cancer stood before me once again and screamed at me that I was going to die. It was as though the cancer was daring me to fight with no hope of winning, just like Goliath did with the Israelites.

Be Determined and Don't Lose Heart (1 Samuel 17:32-38)

When David initially approached Saul about fighting Goliath, Saul discouraged David and said that he couldn't defeat Goliath. David kept insisting and reminded Saul of how he killed both lion and bear when they attacked his sheep. Saul finally agreed to let David fight Goliath.

I needed a determination like David's that I would go out and fight my Goliath called cancer. And just like Saul, many people told me that I could not be victorious unless I did chemotherapy. Nevertheless, I didn't listen to them and reminded myself of all the other times that God had delivered me from previous cancers that invaded my body and soul.

Speak Confidently, Have Unwavering Faith, and Run Toward Goliath (1 Samuel 17:41-50)

David's unwavering belief that God would deliver Goliath into his hands is what led to the death of Goliath. David spoke with confidence that he would defeat Goliath with God's grace and divine power. I, too, needed to have unwavering faith that God would deliver me. I spoke God's Word to my Goliath cancer that stood before me. Words like, "*I shall not die, but live and declare the works of the Lord*" (Psalm 118:17).

Laura's Journey Lesson
Our faith is the stone we throw at our Goliaths to defeat them.

I noticed that David didn't retreat, but rather, he ran toward Goliath. God told me to turn about face and stand firmly on His promises that He would heal me. I ran toward my Goliath called cancer with God's promise knitted deeply around my heart. How could I fail with God on my side? My faith became the stone which I threw at cancer. God did the rest.

2. Be Selective

For all my previous diagnoses, I was open and transparent about sharing information regarding my situation and asking people for prayer. I sensed in my spirit that I needed to be selective this time around. Consequently, there were only seven people that knew the full details about my situation.

God also reminded me of Scriptures about how others' unbelief can prevent someone from receiving a miracle healing (Mark 6:5-6, Matthew 17:19-20, Luke 8:40-42, and Luke 8:49-56). Therefore, I was selective about who

I would let pray with me because I needed a miracle, and I didn't want anyone's unbelief for a miracle to prevent me from receiving my healing.

I started a private prayer group called Living by God's Grace and Divine Power. The purpose of the group was to provide daily support to me by praying God's Word for me. There were four reasons why I wanted people to pray God's Word:

1. To assure me that my requests were in accordance with God's will

2. To increase my faith

3. To feed His promises into my spirit

4. To keep me focused on God and not on my circumstance

At the beginning of each week, I sent a Scripture verse that I asked the group to pray daily. I encouraged them to personalize the verse to me and to study/meditate on the verse throughout the week.

3. Seeking Wise Counsel

As a single Christian woman, I believe that my pastor is my spiritual covering. If I were married, then it would be my husband. I had many decisions to make regarding treatment, and I wanted to meet with my pastor and his wife before I decided anything. I needed my spiritual covering more than anything now.

The day finally arrived for me to meet with them. I shared the background information about my diagnosis with them, and then shared that I had the most peace about doing nothing for treatment and believing God for my miracle. As we continued talking, my pastor said something that became rooted in my spirit. I don't remember his exact words, but he talked about the principle of whatever is in heaven we can have on earth. Healing is in heaven, and it meant that I could be healed on earth. The pastor's wife shared her testimony of how God healed her several years ago from a life-threatening disease. She texted me several healing Scriptures that she stood on while waiting for her healing. We had a wonderful time of prayer before I left. I felt so uplifted. I kept meditating on my pastor's sharing about having on earth what is in heaven.

4. Victory in Spiritual Warfare

I was part of a small group at my church. We met two times per month for Bible study. We began a study by Dr. Tony Evans titled *Victory in Spiritual Warfare* (Evans,

2011) shortly after my fifth diagnosis. God's timing was perfect because I was in a spiritual battle for my life.

The Bible study examined each piece of the armor as described in Ephesians 6:10-17. It was in session five that I heard the principle my pastor talked about – that whatever is in heaven, we can have on earth. Dr. Evans stated that we could grab something from the invisible realm (heaven) and bring it to the visible realm (earth).

My drive home from Bible study headed west into the sunset. The sunset this night was like watching rays of different color lights sparkling in the sky as the red hues settled in. I always listen to worship music while driving. I was almost home when God showed up in my car. As I continued to gaze at the beautiful sunset, He showed me that my healing was in heaven and it was my responsibility to bring it from heaven to earth. Jesus had already done His part; now it was up to me.

Because of my faith studies during the three-month wait between the CT and PET scans, I knew what I had to do to bring my healing from heaven to earth. I had to believe in healing, act like it was so before I saw it, and not let my feelings or circumstances steal it from me. My determination to act, talk, and walk like I was healed before my healing was so strong after my encounter with God that nothing was going to prevent me from receiving my healing. I didn't care what the reports or doctors said; I walked confidently in my belief of receiving my healing.

Laura's Journey Lesson
What is in heaven, we can have on earth. Jesus has done his part. It is up to us to use our faith to bring heavenly gifts to earth.

5. Walking in Obedience

In selecting treatment for my past diagnosis, I always made my decision based on where I had the most peace. For this time around, I only had peace with doing nothing and trusting God for my miracle. Despite this, I still felt the Lord leading me to review my traditional treatment options. Consequently, I decided to seek opinions from three additional doctors. One was located at Baylor's Sammons Cancer Center in Dallas, Texas and the other two were from MD Anderson in Houston, Texas. I had been to both facilities in the past.

My doctor from Baylor wasn't comfortable with me doing nothing and highly suggested chemotherapy. We discussed the matter for about 25 minutes. She also suggested that I return to MD Anderson for a second opinion since I had already been there in the past for my past surgery. This was confirmation for what I had been feeling from the Lord – go to MD Anderson for a second opinion.

I sent a text to my two closest friends about my visit with the doctor at Baylor. One of them immediately responded and said that she wanted to meet with me because she felt she had heard from the Lord regarding my treatment. I was so nervous that she was going to tell me that God wanted me to undergo chemotherapy. I was so relieved when she shared that she too felt God telling her for me not to do chemotherapy and that going to MD Anderson was a great idea.

Because of my work schedule, I couldn't go to MD Anderson for about a month. You may think it strange that I didn't rush to MD Anderson, but one thing I have learned over the years is that cancer has a way of controlling my life. I wasn't going to allow it to control me this time around. I would make the trip when it was convenient for me and not let cancer dictate my schedule.

On June 8, 2017, I met with two doctors from MD Anderson, the first being my primary doctor. We discussed my situation, and he agreed with the treatment options that were presented to me in Dallas, but also wanted to double check to see if the new growth in the lymph node was in an area that could be radiated. He immediately texted the radiologist oncologist, who could meet with me later that afternoon. He also suggested that I consider entering a clinical trial, and he could set up an appointment with the clinical trial nurses immediately after my office visit.

The clinical trial nurses presented me with the information about the trial and told me that I wouldn't be enrolled in the clinical trial until I signed the consent form. I took all the paperwork from them and told them that I would do additional research and get back with them.

Later that afternoon, I met with the radiologist oncologist who reviewed my history with me, who indicated she needed to get additional information from the facility that treated me to know if further radiation was possible.

I returned to Dallas and did my additional research about the clinical trial. I also reviewed the information with my doctor at Baylor, who agreed that it was the best option for me. It seemed like a no-brainer to me.

I called one of the clinical trial nurses and said I was ready to sign the consent form. I told her I could either fax it to her or email it. To my surprise, she said, "We can't accept faxed or email copies. You have to come to MD Anderson to sign it." I asked her how many spots were left. She said, "One, and we have someone else who is interested in enrolling." I told her that I had to be in Houston for work on the following Monday and that I would stop by to sign the consent form. This was on a Wednesday.

I woke up Thursday morning, and didn't have peace about waiting until Monday to sign the consent form. I called the nurse back and told her that I was going to fly to Houston that night and would be in her office at 8 a.m. on Friday to sign the consent form. I made my emergency trip to Houston, signed the consent form, and flew back to Dallas, all within 24 hours.

Signing the consent form only held my spot for me. I wouldn't be fully enrolled in the trial until I passed the pre-clinical trial tests that included blood work, CT scan, two heart tests, and a biopsy.

I returned to MD Anderson on July 10, 2017 for my pre-clinical trial tests. It was a grueling long day. My friend and I returned to the hotel room around 11 p.m.

God Answers My Simple Prayer

I had a private prayer that I didn't share with anyone other than my friend who was with me for the pre-clinical trial tests that day. My prayer was that I would hear the words "no evidence of disease" from the doctor when I met with him after the pre-clinical trial tests the next day.

As my head hit the pillow that Monday night, I told the Lord, "How cool would it be to hear the words 'no evidence of disease' – and the glory that it would bring to Him." I drifted off to sleep.

My appointment was first thing the next morning. I didn't think about my private prayer or my childlike statement that I made to the Lord the night before.

The pre-clinical trial nurse entered the room. She asked if the doctor had been in yet and I said that he had not. She slowly walked over to a chair and sat across the room from me. She said, "Laura, all your tests look good." In my mind, I'm thinking, "Great, that means I can enter the clinical trial." She continued and said, "But, Laura, you will not be able to enter the clinical trial because evidence of disease is a requirement to enter, and your CT scan showed no evidence of disease." I sat stunned and in shock. My friend and I just looked at each other with confusion as to what we had just heard. I asked the nurse to repeat what she had just said, and she did. I then said, "Are you telling me the lymph node that was cancerous in April is no longer cancerous?" She said, "Yes, that is what I'm telling you." I looked at my friend again, and at the same time, we yelled, "Thank you, Jesus." The nurse said, "Yes, thank you, Jesus," and hugged me and then left the room.

The mid-level doctor then entered and handed me the CT scan results and told me the lymph node had shrunk and that my tumor marker numbers were reduced by half. My friend and I again said, "Thank you, Jesus." The primary doctor strolled into the room and said, "I can't explain it, but we'll take it." We then talked about how to proceed from here. My last question to the doctor was, "How often does this happen?" The doctor began shaking his head no and said, "Laura, this doesn't happen here." I went to shake his hand goodbye, but he said: "Oh, no, I'm not shaking your hand. I'm giving you a big hug." He leaned over and gave me a big bear hug.

My friend and I jumped up with excitement and hugged each other as we cried tears of joy for what had just happened. God answered my simple prayer to hear the words **"no evidence of disease."**

Laura's Journey Lesson
We need to create memorials in our lives to remind us of God's goodness and love for us.

Making Memorials

I felt it was important to make memorials that serve as reminders of God's miracle in my life because I knew the devil would try to convince me that I wasn't healed.

The first memorial occurred the evening my friend and I returned from MD Anderson. Several elders and friends met with us to hear the miraculous news of my healing. We had a wonderful time of sharing and praying. Afterward, my friends cut the medical id bracelet from my wrist and wrote the date I was healed (07/11/17) on it, with the words "Healed by God."

I now do this for all my subsequent bracelets from MD Anderson and keep them in my office or carry them with me.

Choose Life. Trust the Lord.

God reminded me again of what He spoke to me before my life-saving surgery a few years earlier. "Choose life. Trust the Lord" was in my mind, along with "Houston saves lives." At this same time, God reminded me of Abraham's willingness to sacrifice his son Isaac and how at the last minute, He stepped in to stop Abraham from doing so.

I understood the first part about choosing life, trusting in the Lord, and that Houston saves lives. − This was God's desire for me to go to Houston so that He could heal me. I originally thought it would be through the clinical trial, but obviously, God had other plans. I didn't fully understand the part about Abraham until after God healed me.

Genesis 22:1 shows that Abraham's story of sacrificing his son was a test of God. How did Abraham respond to the test? With immediate obedience. I'm sure Abraham didn't like the journey God placed him on, but he responded with immediate obedience to begin the journey, trusting that God would work it all out in the end.

Laura's Journey Lesson
In our trials, Jesus expects to find good fruit - not disappointments - in us.

I didn't like my journey either, and I didn't always respond with immediate obedience to the Lord. Nevertheless, I never lost sight of my purpose of growing closer to God and bringing glory to Him. The impact of my test changed me. I became closer to God and allowed Him to shape me into the person that He desired for me to become. I have a greater desire now to declare to others the works of the Lord in my life and to let them know that they too can be healed and set free.

All Things

Romans 8:28 is one of my favorite Scriptures:

"And know that all things work together for good to those who love God, to those who are called according to His purpose."

Laura's Journey Lesson
In our darkest moments, God is always working things for our good even though we can't see it.

My church's worship team writes anointed worship songs and releases CDs of their songs. In January 2017, they sang the song titled "All Things" (Dufrene, 2017) for the first time on the Sunday after I found out about my enlarged lymph node. They sang it a second time three months later, the Sunday after I found out the cancer had returned. This song is about God working out all things in my life even though I cannot see it. Both

Sundays, I cried the entire time the song was played because I was crushed by the news I received. God was the only one that could help me and I needed to believe the lyrics of the song that said, "You are working all things for my good. When I cannot see it, God, I still believe it. You are working all things for my good." I sang the song with my whole heart and told God both times that I believed that good would come from this current situation even though I didn't understand how. I continued to recite Romans 8:28 and sing this song almost daily until I received my miracle in July. My friend and I sang it for almost an hour in the car on the trip home from MD Anderson.

God took my cancer diagnosis, something the devil meant for evil, and worked it for good in my life. I don't know what you are facing, but I do know that if you put your trust in God and stand on His promises, you'll see good come from your darkest moments.

Chapter 7
Overcoming Fear

Face-to-Face with Fear

Fear hit me as soon as I heard the words "you have cancer" for the first time. The fear intensified through my journey and became my traveling companion; it barged into my life like an unwanted guest and took residence deep within my soul. It was during Fall 2015 that fear almost crippled me. Fear was the poison that polluted my soul and brought me to the desolate parched land I was in. I was in a truly dark, lonely place, and it was only by God's grace that I survived and was set free from the fear.

Fear is an issue everyone deals with, regardless of the circumstances we face. Consequently, I decided to include an entire chapter about how God delivered me from the crippling fear that threatened my life. I hope you will allow God to set you free from any fears that hold you captive.

Fear Builds Up

It was after my fourth diagnosis that fear stuck its ugly tentacles deep in my soul. I was so tormented, I felt like jumping out of my skin every time that scan time came around. I knew a positive scan would certainly mean limited treatment options and put me one step closer to dying.

Everyone told me it was normal for cancer patients and survivors to deal with fear and anxiousness. As a child of the most-high God, I knew I didn't need to live my life in torment, and I decided it was time to be free from the annoying torture I felt. The first step to my freedom was admitting to God how bad of a place I was in.

Dried Parch Land

God revealed my spirit and soul were experiencing a dryness like none before. My heart looked like an old dried up prune with no chance of being restored by God's refreshing waters. I cried out to God and asked Him to forgive me for allowing myself to reach this destination. It was a place I didn't want to be, but I was so confused. I wasn't sure how I had arrived here and didn't know my way out. I pleaded with God to lead me out of this desolate place.

Soon after realizing I was in a spiritually dry place, God began showing me the way out. Of course, this involved Him showing me things wrong with my heart.

I felt God leading me to reread a book from many years ago written by Shelia Walsh (Walsh, 2004). One of the first sentences I read stated:

"I had no issue with God, but with me."

Immediately this question popped into my head, "Do you have an issue with God?" To my surprise, the answer was "Yes." I was shocked by my answer. Where did that come from?

I've never blamed God for cancer but I have asked a lot of "Why" questions. Why me? Why did I have to endure? Why did I have to continue with scans, checkups, tests and all the torment that came with it? I was tired. I just wanted to live a normal life without all the suffering.

Normal – what was normal? Other people live with challenges and suffering, but they endure. I wondered if they had the same questions or issues with God.

I didn't want to have an issue with God. I wasn't even sure what my issue was, but I knew I had one and needed to get rid of it. I prayed and asked God to help me get back on the right track. I needed Him more than ever. I so thirsted for lasting victory from the torment I felt. Trusting God was the only way for me to have a lasting victory from the torment. I knew I could sail through life without any worries or fears if I fully trusted God.

I started by asking the question, "What can cancer do to me?" My answer was that cancer could cause me pain, suffering, and, ultimately, death. I continued my soul searching by reading a book written by Joyce Meyer (Meyer, 2004). Joyce provided tips for combating several issues in our lives. As I read three chapters, three separate questions came to me.

Laura's Journey Lesson
We need to reprogram our current equations if they don't line up with Biblical teachings or if they draw our attention away from God.

Straight Talk on Worry

"What was my desire concerning battling cancer?" This was a question that came to mind as I continued to study the section on worry. I desired that I wouldn't have to fight anymore and that I wouldn't be diagnosed with cancer again. This was my desire, but what was God's desire? His desire was for me to be well and healthy and not sick,

but He also desired that I trust in Him and not waiver in my trust. This was God's will – that I completely trust Him with my life no matter what happens to me. How do I get this kind of trust?

Straight Talk on Fear

"Was fear embedded in my thinking process?" This was a question I read in the fear section. My answer shocked me! I came to realize that fear had taken up residency in my soul, and it was crippling and tormenting me. The following equation came to my mind:

$$Cancer = Fear$$

Yes, I was defining cancer as fear. It was like they were best buddies and they both came together as a package. I realized that I needed a new equation.

$$Cancer = Growing\ Closer\ to\ God + Jesus\ Glorified\ Through\ Me$$

Straight Talk on Stress

"Do you believe God is leading you into a place of victory and triumph?" These were words I read in the stress chapter.

My answer to the question was shocking! The word "No" screamed into my soul.

I began to ask myself why I didn't believe God was leading me to a place of victory and triumph. What caused this resounding answer to raise up from the depth of my soul?

I came to realize that I felt like God wanted me just to live a substandard life. You know .... just going through the motions like a ship sailing without direction.

I thought, "How did I get to this place?" I knew my life circumstances from the past few years were challenging and caused me to focus on wrong things at times. I was only surviving and not thriving in the things that God had for me. I came to realize I didn't feel God was leading me to a place of victory and triumph because I was too self-absorbed with my circumstances. I needed to change this. I needed to embrace God's Word and believe it and apply it to my life.

I was so heartbroken by this. I asked God to forgive me and show me the way back to Him.

Getting Back to Green Pastures and Refreshing Waters

Psalm 23:1-3 describes where I needed to go next on my journey:

"The Lord is my shepherd; I shall not want
He makes me to lie down in green pastures;
He leads me beside the still waters.
He restores my soul;
He leads me in the paths of righteousness
For His name's sake."

Oh, how I wanted to be in the Lord's green pastures and sitting beside His still waters. I so needed Him to restore my soul and set me free from the torment of fear.

I decided it was time for me to put on the whole armor of God (Ephesians 6:10-18) and battle back against the enemy who was tormenting me with this fear. I needed a strategy that would create a shift in my thinking and refocus my attention on God.

I began by developing my fear hit list. This was a list of my fears and the actions I needed to take to kill them off one by one. The main fear on my hit list was that cancer would come back, there would be no treatment options, I'd suffer, and eventually die. I felt powerless by all of this, and that was where I made a mistake; I wasn't putting my faith into action to kill off my fears. I needed to let God's divine power rise within me and take control of the situation. Consequently, I took steps to change my thinking and redirect my focus to God.

Changing my thinking occurred by immersing myself in the Word of God. I'd read Scriptures that spoke about my worth and value to God, and how God would use me to minister to others. Additionally, any time I was feeling weak, I'd pull my F.R.O.G coin (see Chapter 4) out of my pocket and reflect about God's goodness and power. Fully relying on God (F.R.O.G.) meant I needed to surrender to God and allow Him to do His will in my life. Eventually, my thinking shifted, and I realized there was a greater purpose for my journey even though I didn't fully understand it.

I ended up in the dry parched land because I did not keep my focus on God and His higher purpose in my life. Things I did to shift my focus back included Bible study, listening to worship music, prayer, and fellowship with other believers.

I wrote Bible verses and Biblical principles on post it notes and pasted them all over my apartment. I shouted them out loud anytime I felt the devil attacking me with fear. I also made a playlist of worship music that specifically addressed being set free from fear or about trusting God in trials. My go-to songs were No Longer Slaves (Bethel Music), Same Power (Jeremy Camp), Break Every Chain (Jesus Culture), and two songs by Tricia Brock - Always and What I Know.

Eventually, I made it back to the land of green pastures and still waters. God set me free from the fear and its torment. I wrote the following entry in my journal after God set me free from the fear.

Monday is scan time again.

I have an overwhelming sense of peace, which is strange because I get very anxious and nervous around my scan times. This peace only comes from my Lord Jesus.

A few months ago, I heard testimony from a friend in my church about his battle with depression. He described his frustration because he would have times where he wasn't depressed, and then depression would hit him and last for months. One time he felt the depression coming, and he asked God a simple question, "Lord, what must I do to be free from depression?" The Lord spoke to him and said, "Give." He has been giving ever since and has been living free from depression.

I heard this testimony about two weeks before my last scan. I was very anxious and nervous because it occurred six months after my treatment, and it seemed all my recurrences were at the six-month mark from either treatment or surgery. The anxiousness and nervousness were so intense, I felt like I would jump out of my skin.

I wanted the same freedom that my church friend experienced from his depression. I decided to ask God what must I do to be free. God's answer was simple and shocking to me, "Believe."

Really? Just believe? That is all I must do?

Although I was shocked at the simplicity of God's answer, I purposed in my heart that I would just believe no matter how I felt. Once I decided this, a peace covered me like a warm blanket and never left me. I studied God's word and spoke it out loud any time anxious thoughts would try to occupy my mind. As I continued to do this, the peace grew deeper into my soul, took root, and never left me. (January 16, 2016)

Don't Worry

God spoke the following words to me in January 2015:

"You can trust in Me.

You don't have to worry or concern yourself with having cancer ever again.

It is finished!"

I wrote this on an index card and posted it in my apartment. I interpreted it as the Lord telling me that cancer would never strike my body again. I was excited and even proclaimed to others that I would never have cancer again.

Laura's Journey Lesson
By trusting God to take care of us, we can live and enjoy our lives to the fullest without worrying about tomorrow's troubles.

You can imagine how confused I was when I received my fourth diagnosis later that year. I said to God, "You told me that I would never have cancer again." I was shocked when He responded, "No, I didn't." I went back to the index card and re-read what He spoke to me. I then saw the spiritual treasure He was trying to tell me. He told me that I didn't "have to worry or concern myself with having cancer ever again." That is a lot different than saying "you won't have cancer ever again." If I put my trust in Him, I didn't need to worry or concern myself with what may happen in the future.

Breaking Free from Fear is Possible

Fear rose within me and took up residence in my soul because of the perceived threat that cancer would come back and I would die. Although this was a real possibility, the perceived threat didn't match reality because I had removed God from the equation. With God, all things are possible, even a miraculous healing when no conventional treatment options are available. In my case, I broke free from fear because I finally came to a place of acceptance that whatever the outcome, I would not worry about the future. I lived my life one day at a time and enjoyed every single day.

I don't know what fears you are facing, but I do know you can experience freedom from them just like I did. Freedom comes by taking the first step in deciding you want to be free, asking God to help you develop your battle plan, and then walking it out.

Chapter 8
Finding Spiritual Treasures Through Cancer

All Things
October 10, 2012

"And we know all things work together for good to those who love God, to those called according to His purpose." Romans 8:28

God's word is the truth. This Scripture tells me that all things work together for my good. I may not be able to see the good right now in the journey that I'm on, but I believe good will come from it.

When my emotions started to go wild today, I brought myself back to this Scripture and focused on the good that will come to me and others. My emotions calmed, and peace came returned. I am thankful for God's peace.

> ***Spiritual Treasure****: What the devil meant for evil, God meant for good, even though I may not see it when I'm going through trials.*

Why Road

October 11, 2012

"Trust in the Lord with all your heart, and lean not on your own understanding; In all ways acknowledge Him, and He shall direct your path." Proverbs 3:5-6

This Scripture I memorized in my early days of accepting Jesus into my heart. I call it my "Why Road" Scripture. In difficult times, it is natural for me to ask the question "Why?" The problem with this question is that it leads me down a path that only causes confusion, frustration, and anxiety. Consequently, a long time ago, I decided not to travel down the "Why Road," but rather trust in the Lord, lean not to my own understanding, and acknowledge that God is still sovereign despite my circumstances. My experiences show me God directs my path and His peace fills my soul when I do this.

Spiritual Treasure: The "Why Road" leads to confusion, frustration, and anxiety. I must not lean on my own understanding, but rather acknowledge God and He will direct my road to travel.

Meditating on God's Word
October 12, 2012

"How precious are Your thoughts to me, O God! How great is the sum of them! If I should count them, they would be more than the number in the sand. When I awake, I am still with You."
Psalm 139:17-18

When I was going through another trial in life several years ago, a friend recommended I read Psalm 139 daily. I did for about six months, and it transformed my life! This Psalm is about God's perfect knowledge of me from beginning to end. How wonderful it is that God knows me better than I know me. This diagnosis didn't take Him by surprise – He knew about it even before I was born. When I feel anxious about the days ahead, I can rest in knowing that He is watching over me and will be with me.

I'm thankful that I took my friend's suggestion to read Psalm 139 daily. It was "spiritual boot camp" to prepare me for where I am today. God's strength sustained me then and will sustain me now.

> ***Spiritual Treasure****: Meditation on God's Word will help me through my trials. It will also help me keep my focus on God.*

Give Thanks and Praise God
October 16, 2012

"...giving thanks always for all things to God the Father in the name of our Lord Jesus Christ." Ephesians 5:20

It has been seven days since being diagnosed with cancer. One thing remains: I give thanks and praise God through the storm. How do I do this? Because God is worthy of my praise and thanksgiving; He is the almighty, the beginning and the end, sovereign, and my circumstance doesn't change who He is.

During church this past Sunday, I ran to the altar worshiping Him. God met me there and ministered to me as I poured my heart to Him. I am so thankful for His presence and the people who came to me to be used by God to show me His love and comfort.

I'm thankful for all of you participating in this group. I routinely check the group posts throughout the day. Your prayers, comments, and posts bring me such comfort and strength to continue walking this journey out. I so appreciate you and love you. Thank you.

Regardless of what is ahead for me, I will always give thanks and praise God. I'm so glad that I have a personal relationship with God through Jesus. I couldn't imagine walking this road without Him. Thank you, thank you, Lord.

> **Spiritual Treasure**: *Giving thanks and praise to God during my storm allows God to enter the storm and bring me calm and peace.*

God's Higher Purpose
October 19, 2012

"He went a little farther and fell on His face, and prayed, saying 'O My Father, if it possible, let this cup pass from Me; nevertheless, not as I will, but as You will." Matthew 26:39

This was Jesus' prayer in the Garden before being crucified on the cross. He prayed the same prayer two other times; see verses 42 and 44.

I can't count how many times I've prayed this same prayer since being diagnosed with cancer, "Yes, Lord, let this cancer pass from me, nevertheless not as I will, but as You will."

Just as Jesus realized in the Garden, God has a higher purpose for me to walk this journey out. Yes, God can take this cancer from me today, and that would be wonderful! But would that fulfill His higher purpose?

I think about what if God had answered Jesus' prayer in the Garden and let the crucifixion pass from Jesus. How my life would be so empty without Jesus and how I would have to walk this journey without God; I can't even imagine what it would be like walking this out without God. Yes it can be scary and hopeless. I'm thankful that God didn't let the cup pass Jesus. I'm thankful that Jesus was obedient to the Father so I can now experience God's presence in my life. Nevertheless, I am sorry that Jesus went through all the pain and suffering for my benefit.

Today I will be having a CT scan to determine if cancer has migrated out of the uterus into any other of my organs. Regardless of the results, I know God is with me and that He has a higher purpose for me going through this trial.

> *Spiritual Treasure: God has a higher purpose for my storms, and my focus needs to be on His higher purpose rather than my storms.*

God's Time is Perfect
October 20, 2012

It didn't take long for the tears to begin flowing when I got back in the car after my CT scan yesterday. My thoughts were, "God, how could I handle the news if the CT shows that cancer has spread. I am emotionally weak and can't take much more." My friend grabbed my hand and asked me what was going on inside of me. I shared my thoughts with her. She then said, "That is a bridge that hasn't come yet." I said, "I know, but I'm tired of crossing bridges." Later in the day, she prayed that God would infuse me with His presence and give me strength.

It was interesting that Sarah Young's devotion that I read earlier today talked about weaknesses and used the exact word (infuse) that my friend used in her prayer. (Young, 2011) The timing of the Lord is always perfect to encourage me to carry on and give me strength. Yes, I will have weak moments, but it is a prelude to God infusing energy into my being. My prayer is, "Lord, I'm ready to be infused, come give me your daily dose of strength so that I may boldly continue."

Spiritual Treasure: God's timing is perfect for all aspects of my life. He will provide exactly what I need at the exact time that I need it.

Living Abundantly Amidst the Storms

October 26, 2012

"The thief does not come except to steal, and to kill, and to destroy. I have come that they may have life, and that they may have it more abundantly." John 10:10

This verse is part of a parable Jesus shared to distinguish between false shepherds and a true shepherd, Jesus. The devil is a false shepherd, and his sole purpose is to steal, kill, and destroy me. He will use any means he can to draw me away from the true shepherd Jesus.

In challenging seasons like the one I'm in now, it would be easy for me to think I can't experience an abundant life through it all. This is exactly what the devil would want me to think. Nevertheless, I choose to think that I can live an abundant life through it and experience the fullness that Christ offers. Did you notice I said, "Choose?" Choosing what I think about during this time determines whether I have life and have it more abundantly. My circumstance doesn't change who God is, and I won't let my thinking change either. Living the abundant life is available to me at all times, and I choose to live it regardless of my circumstance.

> ***Spiritual Treasure:*** *If I choose, I can live an abundant life with joy and peace amidst my storms.*

Growing Spiritually During Storms
October 30, 2012

"And He said to me, 'My grace is sufficient for you, for My strength is made perfect in weakness.' Therefore, most gladly I will rather boast in my infirmities, that the power of Christ may rest upon me." 2 Corinthians 12:9

This is a verse from a person at church on Sunday. The verse shows God's response to Paul's prayer request to take his infirmity away. Paul describes this infirmity as a "thorn in the flesh" (verse 7) and how he requested three times for God to take it from him (verse 8).

God's response shows that He would give Paul the grace to deal with the infirmity rather than take it from him. On the surface, this seems like a harsh response to Paul, but Paul's response to God shows that he would rather have the power of Christ (grace) rest upon him to deal with the infirmity. Paul chose to accept God's response and His grace to deal with it. I am making the same choice.

It would be wonderful for God to instantly heal me from cancer and to avoid surgery and treatments; I know God is able, but I'm content if He decides a different course of healing for me. For I know His grace (power of Christ) is with me. I also know God's purpose is bigger than mine. Barnes Commentary states, "The removal of the calamity might be apparently a blessing, but it might also be attended with danger to our spiritual welfare; the grace imparted may be of permanent value and may relate to the loveliest traits of Christian character" (Barnes, 1962).

I desire to grow spiritually through this circumstance and become more Christ like during the journey. God's grace is an ingredient in His recipe for my life to help me achieve this. Thank you, Lord, for Your grace. May Your strength be made perfect in my weakness.

Spiritual Treasure: God's grace is sufficient for getting me through my storms. His grace allows me to grow spiritually through the storms.

A Thankful Heart and Praise God
October 30, 2012

"Enter His gates with thanksgiving and his courts with praise; give thanks to Him and praise His name." Psalm 100:4

I usually write and post my God treatments at the beginning of each day. Since I wouldn't be able to do this the day after my surgery, I am writing this treatment one day ahead of time (October 30). This means that I don't know the outcomes or results of my surgery.

I selected today's God treatment because I will always enter God's presence with a thankful heart and praise Him regardless of my circumstance. My circumstance, or in this case the surgery outcome/result, doesn't change who God is, and He is worthy of all my praise and thanksgiving regardless of the outcome/result. Please join me, give Him praise, and thank Him for watching over me.

> **Spiritual Treasure**: *My thankfulness and praise of God are independent of the outcome of my circumstances. God is worthy of praise always!*

Focus on Jesus

November 9, 2012

Sarah Young's devotion for today talks about the importance of appreciating difficult days and that with God I can handle anything. (Young, 2011) I've experienced many challenges in the past few days and haven't been able to post my God treatments. It all began Monday night when I began running a fever. The fever persisted and increased throughout the day on Tuesday. This combined with experiencing the worst pain since my surgery confined me to my bed or couch for most of the day.

Today's devotion reminds me to keep my focus on Jesus during difficult times. This focus comes through personal worship time, reading the Bible, and meditating on how God was with me and brought me through past difficult times. Despite how bad I feel, it is my responsibility to keep my focus on Jesus and seeking Him. In doing this, I will get through the difficult days with Jesus being with me every step of the way.

> ***Spiritual Treasure:*** *I get through the storms by keeping my focus on Jesus. Key ways for me to keep my focus include praise and worship, reading the Bible, and prayer.*

Gaining Wisdom Through Trials
November 13, 2012

*"If any of you lacks wisdom, let him ask of God, who gives
to all liberally and without reproach, and it will be given to
him." James 1:5*

As I survey my life, I realize I've gained more wisdom
during trials. Why is this? It is because trials expose my
weaknesses, I see my need for God more, and diligently
seek Him. I yield myself to God so He can work in my
life during trials and I ask Him for wisdom in what I
need to do. I'm thankful that God generously gives
wisdom when I ask. His wisdom far surpasses mine.

Spiritual Treasure: *Gaining more of God's wisdom
is a benefit that I can experience through storms, provided I
ask God for it.*

Victories in Storms

November 17, 2012

Asking God for victories is not a common thing I do. When I'm faced with trials, I usually seek God and hope for the best.

The victory wasn't even a thought when I first received the news about cancer. Matter of fact my thoughts were just the opposite – defeated. All I could think about was how I needed God more than ever. I didn't ask or look for victory. I looked for God from the beginning. Perhaps my seeking was a way of me asking God for victory.

I am thankful for God's victories and miracles in my life. In the future, I plan on asking Him for more victories, seeking Him, and waiting for His miracles to unfold in my life.

> **Spiritual Treasure**: *Seeking God as I wait for Him to bring victories during my storms results in miracles.*

Attitude is Everything
November 19, 2012

"It's not our circumstances that steal our joy, it's the way we think about them." (Hagee, 2012)

The above statement appeared on John Hagee Ministries' Facebook page this morning.

Webster defines attitude as: "an organismic state of readiness to respond characteristically to a stimulus (as an object, concept, or situation)."

"State of readiness" implies that I've predetermined the posture I'll take when faced with trials – posture meaning how I think and respond.

The statement posted on John Hagee Ministries' Facebook page shows that my thinking influences my response to life trials. My thinking is shaped by my attitude. My attitude is determined by my trust and faith in God. A strong trust and faith in God is the way I maintain a positive "state of readiness" and have a positive attitude as I face cancer.

> *Spiritual Treasure: My attitude shapes the way I respond to storms. My way of thinking about my trials shapes my attitude. A strong trust and faith in God is the way to maintain a positive attitude.*

God Will Deliver Me from My Goliath
November 16, 2013

The past two mornings have been very challenging for me. Fear and worry greeted me as soon as I opened my eyes. These were not feelings that motivated me to jump out of bed with the strength to face the day ahead. Nevertheless, I got up and resolved to carry on my normal activities despite the fear and worry consuming my mind.

It didn't take long for the flood of tears to come after getting up. My tears cried out to God. Tears associated with the unanswered question of "Why?", tears crying out in fear and worry, tears of desperation. These were all tears that expressed my true feelings to God about my circumstance. Despite my tears, I continued on with my morning.

I like to swim or workout when I first get up. I often find that God ministers to me during these times. Yesterday and today, I experienced God in ways that only He knew I needed. The experience I'll share is what happened today; perhaps I'll share yesterday's experience later.

I felt compelled to walk rather than swim this morning. I headed out the door with my earphones and music. It wasn't long into the walk before the tears began to flow again and I cried out to God. Something amazing happened; He gave me a vision. The vision was of Jesus walking ahead of me with an army of angels on both sides of Him. There were also two angels standing on either side of me. I heard the Lord say, "Laura, I am walking ahead of you, clearing the way for you to walk through this circumstance." The angels beside me encouraged me to walk with strength and to keep looking to Jesus as He walked ahead of me. This vision brought to mind the story of David and Goliath.

1 Samuel 17:48 states:

"So it was, when the Philistine (Goliath) arose and came and drew near to meet David, that David hurried and ran toward the army to meet the Philistine."

Notice that David didn't hesitate, but ran toward Goliath with confidence and boldness that he would be victorious. How was he able to do this? Because he knew his God and trusted Him to deliver Goliath into his hands. Earlier in 1 Samuel 17:45-47 David told Goliath:

"... You come to me with a sword, with a spear, and with a javelin. But I come to you in the name of the Lord of hosts, the God of the armies of Israel, whom you have defied. This day the Lord will deliver you into my hand, and I will strike you and take your head from you. And this day I will give the carcasses of the camp of the Philistines to the birds of the air and the wild beasts of the earth, that all the earth may know that there is a God in Israel. Then all this assembly shall know that the Lord does not save with sword and spear; for the battle is the Lord's, and He will give you into our hands."

Cancer is the Goliath in my life right now. Despite my feelings of fear and worry, I need to run toward this Goliath with confidence and boldness, knowing that through God I will be victorious. God is going before me with His army; the battle is the Lord's, and He will deliver me from this cancer.

> ***Spiritual Treasure***: *I can approach storms with confidence and boldness knowing that through God I will be victorious. God will go before me with His army; the battle will be the Lord's and He will deliver me from my storms.*

Excitement in the Storms

August 14, 2014

"You do not know about tomorrow. What is your life? For you are a puff of smoke that appears for a short time and then vanishes."
James 4:14 (NET)

It is vacation time! I'm enjoying God's beautiful creation in the Rocky Mountains. As I type, I hear the roaring creek flow, and I am watching the sunrise. Such beauty to enjoy.

A few weeks ago, I began to think about my vacation time in the Rocky Mountains. An excitement exploded in my soul. I didn't understand this excitement. I felt like a little child preparing for the first vacation of my life. What would I see? What new experiences would I encounter? Who would I meet? How many miles would I travel? What wonderful food would my stomach enjoy? These were all questions that arose in my childlike mind during my excitement.

As my friend and I traveled from Texas through New Mexico to Colorado, I began to understand my excitement.

Looking back 5½ months ago, when I completed my last radiation treatment, my mindset was to get through treatment one day at a time. I also learned not to take anything for granted, live life in the present, and enjoy every second of my life.

This exploding excitement I feel is rooted in the fact that I know where I was 5½ months ago and now I get to experience life knowing that God brought me through. I don't know what tomorrow will bring or the next day, as James 4:14 states. But, I know this: I'm thankful for every day that God gives me, and I enjoy living one day at a time.

Spiritual Treasure: *Thankfulness for what God brings me through leads to excitement to live all the days of my life to the fullest.*

Anniversary Dates

September 22, 2015

Tomorrow is a special day for two reasons.

A year ago tomorrow, I underwent a life-saving surgery to remove a cancerous tumor from my body. I received the best surgery outcome possible considering my situation. The tumor was contained, and no cancer was detected in my lymph nodes. Even though my recovery was long, I fully expected to live the rest of my life cancer free. After all, this was the third time I had battled it in two years.

A CT and PET scan six months after my surgery confirmed cancer in two of my lymph nodes. Although this news initially devastated and crippled me, I resolved in my heart to keep standing on God's word and fight this disease that has been trying to destroy me. I underwent five weeks of radiation treatment for 5 days each week. My first scan after treatment confirmed that the treatment worked and the doctors told me that the cancer was in remission.

Tomorrow is my six-month scan following radiation; this is the 2nd reason why tomorrow is special. The timing of the scan – on my surgery anniversary date – is by God's design.

Why?

I hate when my scans roll around every three months. It is almost like I get on an emotional roller coaster ride and my mind entertains all the wrong thoughts. This time has been different. Because of the timing of the scan, I've read my posts up to and after my surgery. This has instilled the same confidence and trust in God that I felt last year going into the surgery. God was with me then, and He will be with me tomorrow and the next day when I get the results.

I'm fully believing and praying for a clear scan. Please join me in prayer for this outcome. Please also pray that I will keep my eyes fully fixed on God over the next two days because I don't like the emotional roller coaster ride with my mind thinking about wrong thoughts.

Spiritual Treasure: God is always with me regardless of what challenges I face

F.R.O.G. Makes a Difference

September 27, 2015

God uses anything to drive me closer to Him. Even a picture of a frog.

I was at a doctor's office a couple of weeks before my recent CT scan. As I was leaving the room, a picture of a frog grabbed my attention. It was screaming at me, "Do you remember the meaning of F.R.O.G?" Oh! How I had forgotten about F.R.O.G.!

I was introduced to the meaning of F.R.O.G. about a year ago when I was at MD Anderson getting a second opinion about my surgery. I was on the shuttle riding to my appointment when a man handed me a coin. The coin had a picture of a frog on it with F.R.O.G. written on the top and "Fully Rely on God" written on the bottom. The Scripture reference to Isaiah 26:4 with the words "Fully Rely on God" were printed on the back of the coin.

I carried the coin in my pocket every day for several months. Any time I felt uncertain about my future and fear came upon me, I'd pull the coin out and was reminded that I could trust God no matter what. I lost the coin, and it became a distant memory.

After I saw the picture of the frog in the doctor's office, I longed to have my coin back because it was my six-month scan after my last treatment. My past experiences have been that a recurrence happens six months after treatment or surgery. I knew how critical this scan was and I didn't want history to repeat itself. Of course, the devil was right there, always reminding me of my history.

When I got home from the doctor's office, I tore my apartment apart looking for the coin. I didn't find it and then decided to order another one online. I received ten coins in the mail about two weeks before my scan.

After I received my new coins, I began to meditate on what it means to rely on God. I went to my Bible and studied Isaiah 26:3-4:

"You will keep him in perfect peace, Whose mind is stayed on You, Because he trusts in You. Trust in the Lord forever, For in Yah, the Lord, is everlasting strength."

Keep me in perfect peace despite the fear I was facing. How does this happen? By keeping my mind stayed on God because I trust in Him. A mind that has confidence in God shall not be agitated by trials. I made a conscious decision early last week that I wasn't going to allow the devil to torment me anymore and steal the perfect peace I was entitled to. I took back what the enemy stole from me by battling the devil with God's Word. Any time I was feeling weak, I'd pulled my coin out of my pocket and I was reminded I could trust God no matter what.

It was amazing to me the amount of peace I had the day of my scan and when I got the results the next day. Out of all my scans I've ever had, last week's scan was the best. The radiologists report indicated there was no evidence of progressing or new disease present. I've never had a report like that. Thank you, Lord!

> **Spiritual Treasure**: *I can have perfect peace in my storms by keeping my mind stayed on God.*

Shine Your Light

July 8, 2017

"A man's heart plans his way, But the Lord directs his steps."
(Proverbs 16:9)

I have been exploring different options for God's course of direction regarding the most recent cancer diagnosis I received in April. After seeing multiple doctors and extensive prayer, I've decided to enter a clinical trial at MD Anderson in Houston, Texas. The trial provides a targeted therapy designed only to impact cancer. This means side effects are minimal, which I'm very happy about.

A friend and I will be traveling to MD Anderson tomorrow and will be there until Wednesday. I'll undergo a series of tests on Monday and Tuesday and will meet with a lot of doctors. After next week, I'll got to MD Anderson once a week for three weeks and then once a month after that.

Matthew 5:15-16 states:

"Nor do they light a lamp and put it under a basket, but on a lampstand, and it gives light to all who are in the house. 16 Let your light so shine before men, that they may see your good works and glorify your Father in heaven." Matthew 5:15-16

Since hearing the words "you have cancer" for the fifth time, I have purposed in my heart to let my light shine before others and be a witness for God. I ask for your prayers to continue to have opportunities to shine for Him during my time at MD Anderson.

I appreciate all of you and your support through this journey. Although I wish I were at the end of the journey, I'm not. God has other plans, and He is directing my steps.

Spiritual Treasure: I can shine my light brightly despite the darkness surrounding me.

Rejoice

July 11, 2017

Philippians 4:4 states, *"Rejoice in the Lord always. Again I say, rejoice!"*

I have much to rejoice about this morning. After going through a series of tests yesterday, my doctor shared the same words that I had asked God for: "There is no evidence of disease in your body." Yes, I am healed by God, and I am rejoicing and singing praises to Him. Please rejoice with me and give praises to His name.

Spiritual Treasure: God heals!

Thanking God
October 27, 2017

I've thought about writing a thank you letter to God for giving me my miracle. The only words I can find to write are in Psalm 118:17: "I shall not die but live and declare the works of the Lord." All I can say is that I'm thankful to God and will forever declare His works in my life.

> ***Spiritual Treasure****: It is good to thank the Lord for His mighty works in my life and share with others what the Lord has done.*

Chapter 9
Medical Evidence for My Miracle

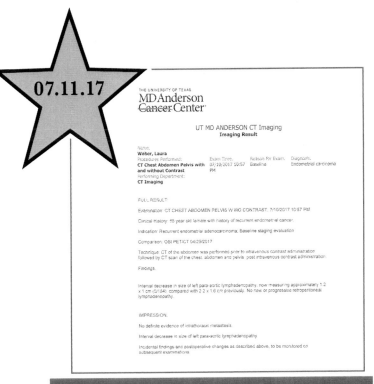

07.11.17

THE UNIVERSITY OF TEXAS
MD Anderson
~~Cancer~~ Center

UT MD ANDERSON CT Imaging
Imaging Result

Name:
Weber, Laura
Procedures Performed: Exam Time: Reason for Exam: Diagnosis:
CT Chest Abdomen Pelvis with   07/10/2017 10:57   Baseline   Endometrial carcinoma
and without Contrast   PM
Performing Department:
CT Imaging

FULL RESULT

Examination: CT CHEST ABDOMEN PELVIS W WO CONTRAST, 7/10/2017 10:57 PM

Clinical History: 55 year old female with history of recurrent endometrial cancer.

Indication: Recurrent endometrial adenocarcinoma; Baseline staging evaluation

Comparison: OSI PET/CT 04/25/2017

Technique: CT of the abdomen was performed prior to intravenous contrast administration
followed by CT scan of the chest, abdomen and pelvis post intravenous contrast administration.

Findings:

Interval decrease in size of left para-aortic lymphadenopathy, now measuring approximately 1.2
x 1 cm (5/184), compared with 2.2 x 1.6 cm previously. No new or progressive retroperitoneal
lymphadenopathy.

IMPRESSION:

No definite evidence of intrathoracic metastasis.

Interval decrease in size of left para-aortic lymphadenopathy.

Incidental findings and postoperative changes as described above, to be monitored on
subsequent examinations.

**"No evidence of recurrence
or metastatic disease."**

When I met Laura in September 2014, she was in
the hospital recovering from her pelvic exenteration
surgery. I was working two jobs. My full-time
job as a gynecologist for Texas Oncology at the
Sammons Cancer Center involved assisting the

135

cancer gynecologists (gynecologist oncologists) with postoperative hospital visits and in office surveillance appointments. I treated people with pre-invasive disease (abnormal Pap testing or irregular bleeding) and helped with diagnostic surgeries. I also set up a survivorship program to assist patients after their treatments were completed. It was in this role that I met Laura. I don't remember the particulars of that meeting (I was covering four hospitals and two doctors for postoperative rounds). What struck me, though, was her determination to move out of the bed and improve her strength and stamina.

My second job was through the Baylor Integrative and Functional Medicine program. When she established in this practice in 2015, we spent the first appointment talking for 90 minutes about her medical history and reviewing emotional, mental, physical and spiritual health. We discussed nutrition and stress management. She had a clear picture of her medical and cancer history with four recurrences of uterine cancer and was looking for additional support. Ultimately, we decided on acupuncture treatments along with some nutritional testing. Every time she had a CT or PET scan or blood work through her "traditional" gynecologist oncologist, we would review them and process them together.

When a possible recurrence of her cancer showed up
in her blood work and CT/PET scan for the fifth time,
I strongly agreed with her decision to get additional
opinions. We discussed all of the options together.
One option was a clinical trial at MD Anderson; I
reviewed the clinical trial paperwork and researched
the chemotherapy agent and its action so I could better
explain it to her. I wondered why the MD Anderson
doctors felt it was necessary to repeat the scans – the
radiation exposure was concerning to me but now, in
retrospect, I'm grateful they did!

I was shocked, amazed and grateful to learn that the
repeat scans and blood work at MD Anderson showed
no evidence of disease. I can't think of a time I have seen
this happen before. Healing grace had filled her up; she
shines for all of us to see and rejoice.

Claudia E. Harsh, MD

My Cancer Diagnosis Timeline

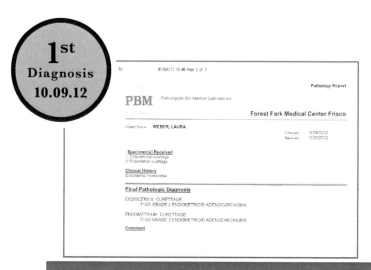

1st Diagnosis 10.09.12

To: 01/0ct/12 15:00 Page 2 of 7

Pathology Report

PBM Pathologists, Bio-Medical Laboratories

Forest Fark Medical Center Frisco

Patient Name   WEBER, LAURA

Collected   9/28/2012
Received   9/28/2012

Specimen(s) Received
1. Endocervical curettage
2. Endometrial curettage

Clinical History
Endometrial Hyperplasia

Final Pathologic Diagnosis

ENDOCERVIX. CURETTAGE:
    FIGO GRADE 2 ENDOMETRIOID ADENOCARCINOMA

ENDOMETRIUM. CURETTAGE:
    FIGO GRADE 2 ENDOMETRIOID ADENOCARCINOMA

Comment

Endometrial Adenocarcinoma

Treatment:
Surgery followed by 4 high dose radiation treatments

138

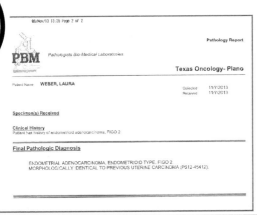

06/Nov/13 13:39 Page 2 of 2

Pathology Report

Pathologists Bio-Medical Laboratories

Texas Oncology- Plano

Patient Name WEBER, LAURA

Collected   11/7/2013
Received   11/7/2013

Specimen(s) Received

Clinical History
Patient has history of endometrioid adenocarcinoma, FIGO 2

Final Pathologic Diagnosis

ENDOMETRIAL ADENOCARCINOMA, ENDOMETRIOID TYPE, FIGO 2
MORPHOLOGICALLY IDENTICAL TO PREVIOUS UTERINE CARCINOMA (PS12-45412).

Endometrial Adenocarcinoma - Identical to previous Uterine Carcinoma

Treatment:
Radiation 5 days/week for 5 weeks followed by
3 high-dose radiation treatments

09/26/2014 at 18:00:47 - from - to p9/10

WEBER, LAURA J.   PHD HISTOLOGY REPORT

p53   Negative

Sections (A25) demonstrate a small focus of metastatic adenocarcinoma.

Sections (A26, A27) of right and left ureter are unremarkable.

Full thickness sections of bladder demonstrate focal adenocarcinoma (A32) adjacent to the left ureteral orifice.

Sections (A34-A40) demonstrate three small benign lymph nodes.   No metastatic tumor is seen.

(lp/crg/ft)

Diagnosis

PELVIC EXENTERATION:

    METASTATIC ENDOMETRIAL ADENOCARCINOMA, ENDOMETRIOID TYPE.
    RESECTION MARGINS NOT INVOLVED

BLADDER, RADICAL CYSTECTOMY:
    METASTATIC ENDOMETRIAL ADENOCARCINOMA INVOLVING PERIURETERAL ORIFICE.
    URETERAL AND SOFT TISSUE RESECTION MARGINS NOT INVOLVED.

PELVIC LYMPH NODES:
    THREE SMALL LYMPH NODES IDENTIFIED.
    NO METASTATIC CARCINOMA SEEN

Metastatic Endometrial Adenocarcinoma

Treatment:

Surgery

4th
Diagnosis
03.18.15

IMAGING REPORT
TEXAS RADIOLOGY ASSOCIATES, LLP

Patient: Name: Laura Weber

Order:
        Date   3/18/2015 8:12 AM
        Procedure: PET/CT

PLANO WEST CANCER CENTER
TEXAS RADIOLOGY ASSOCIATES, LLP
CONSULTING RADIOLOGISTS

PATIENT NAME: Laura Weber

EXAM: PET/CT from 3/18/2015 8:45 AM

HISTORY: Uterine cancer

TECHNIQUE: Approximately 1 hour after the injection of 14.2 mCi of F-18 FDG, whole body PET/CT was performed from the skull base to the mid thighs. The patient's blood glucose level was 83 mg/dl. CT was performed primarily for attenuation correction and anatomic localization. Images were reviewed on an independent GE workstation.

COMPARISON: PET/CT from June 30, 2014. CT from February 26, 2015.

Impression:

2 metastatic left abdominal retroperitoneal lymph nodes with maximum SUV of 5.7.

Endometrial Carcinoma - Two metastatic left abdominal retroperitoneal lymph nodes

---

Treatment:
Radiation treatment, 5 days/week for 5 weeks; hormonal treatment
1 pill/day forever

141

5th
Diagnosis
04.25.17

IMAGING REPORT
TEXAS RADIOLOGY ASSOCIATES, LLP

Patient: Name: Laura Weber

Order:
          Date: 4/25/2017 10:17 AM
          Procedure: PET/CT

PLANO WEST CANCER CENTER
TEXAS RADIOLOGY ASSOCIATES, LLP
CONSULTING RADIOLOGISTS

PATIENT NAME: Laura Weber

EXAM: PET/CT from 4/25/2017 10:17 AM

HISTORY: Uterine cancer. Restaging.

TECHNIQUE: Approximately 1 hour after the injection of 12.3 mCi of F-18 FDG, whole body PET/CT was performed from the skull base to the mid thighs. The patient's blood glucose level was 88 mg/dl. CT was performed primarily for attenuation correction and anatomic localization. Images were reviewed on an independent workstation. ALARA principles followed.

COMPARISON: PET/CT from 3/18/2015. CT from 1/23/2017

FINDINGS:

Further increase in the metastatic left periaortic lymph node now measuring 2.1 cm with a maximum SUV of 18.6. On the prior CT this measured 1.4 cm. No other metabolically active lymph node is identified. There is no FDG evidence for osseous or hepatic metastatic disease. There is no metabolically active lung parenchymal abnormality. There is no FDG evidence for omental, peritoneal, or mesenteric metastatic disease.

Impression:

Enlarging highly metabolically active metastatic left periaortic lymph node.
Maximum SUV is 18.6.

Endometrial Carcinoma - Enlarging highly metabolically active metastatic left periaortic lymph node

Treatment:
None.
Doctor stopped hormonal treatment.

07.11.17

UT MD ANDERSON CT Imaging
Imaging Result

Name:
Weber, Laura
Procedures Performed: Exam Time: Reason for Exam: Diagnosis:
CT Chest Abdomen Pelvis with   07/10/2017 10:57   Baseline   Endometrial carcinoma
and without Contrast   PM
Performing Department:
CT Imaging

FULL RESULT:

Examination: CT CHEST ABDOMEN PELVIS W WO CONTRAST. 7/10/2017 10:57 PM

Clinical History: 55 year old female with history of recurrent endometrial cancer.

Indication: Recurrent endometrial adenocarcinoma. Baseline staging evaluation

Comparison: OSI PET/CT 04/29/2017

Technique: CT of the abdomen was performed prior to intravenous contrast administration followed by CT scan of the chest, abdomen and pelvis post intravenous contrast administration.

Findings:

Interval decrease in size of left para-aortic lymphadenopathy, now measuring approximately 1.2 x 1 cm (S/18.4), compared with 2.2 x 1.6 cm previously. No new or progressive retroperitoneal lymphadenopathy.

IMPRESSION:

No definite evidence of intrathoracic metastasis.

Interval decrease in size of left para-aortic lymphadenopathy.

Incidental findings and postoperative changes as described above, to be monitored on subsequent examinations.

**"No evidence of recurrence
or metastatic disease."**

143

Acknowledgments

Many people helped me through my journey. Their support allowed me to write this book.

I thank God for allowing me to go through the journey. He was with me all the time, even when I didn't know it. My faith grew during the journey. I know things about God that I otherwise wouldn't have learned without the journey. After my fifth diagnosis, I prayed the following prayer everyday "I shall not die, but live and declare the works of the Lord." I wrote this book to declare God's miraculous works in my life because I live. I dedicate this book to my Lord and Savior Jesus Christ. May He be glorified through my writing.

I recognize that my early faith walk at Christian Fellowship Center in Madrid, NY was key for planting deep roots of Bible faith in me, which was crucial for me remaining steadfast during the most challenging times. I'm thankful to Pastor Rick and Darlene Sinclair for investing in me during the early years of my Christian walk. Your investment provided the solid faith foundation for me to stand upon during my battle.

I thank Pastor Ricky and Cyd Texada. They are my current pastors at Covenant Church - Colleyville, TX.

Your faith is contagious, and your love for God shines brightly. Your continuing ministry to me and constant prayers stir my faith to remain strong in the battle. Our meeting before my first appointment at MD Anderson in June 2017 was instrumental in giving me the strength to go in faith that God would heal me. Thank you for showing me that we can have heavenly healing here on earth.

I thank my family (Dad, Mom, Wayne, Karen, and Clark) for walking with me. I don't realize what a toll my cancer journey was for you all. All the tears and sleepless nights. I know my journey was harder for you than it was for me at times. Nevertheless, you continued to love and encourage me through it all. I especially want to thank my brother, Wayne, for making all the phone calls after my many diagnoses when I couldn't make them, and for allowing me to use your photograph for the cover of my book.

I'm grateful for the many people that provided practical help during my journey. These people either provided meals, drove me to my appointments and treatments, and stayed by my side during surgeries. I especially am grateful to Kay Zimmerman, Cathy Allen, and Debbie

Sharp for all of their sacrifices they made. May God richly bless you for your service to me.

I am truly blessed to be working for a great employer (The Lane Construction Corporation). My first diagnosis occurred three months after I started working for them. Their message to me was "go take care of yourself, and your job will be here when you return." With each subsequent diagnosis, their message remained the same. I am grateful for their support and couldn't have made it through without them.

I wouldn't be here today without the great care from my team of doctors and treatment technicians. I am truly grateful to them all for providing me the best medical care that I could have asked for.

I thank Cuisine for Healing (www.cuisineforhealing. org) for showing me the importance of proper nutrition needed for battling cancer. You all are family to me, and I look forward to helping you fulfill your mission of providing nutritious, delicious food to people combating life-threatening diseases.

I especially appreciate Dr. Claudia Harsh. I was at my lowest when we first met. Your holistic approach to my care and treatment brought me to a place of healing and wholeness. I am grateful for all that you did for me and thank you for writing the introduction to Chapter 9.

I am grateful to Julie Shaffer of Shaffer Creative (www. shaffercreative.com) for designing my book cover and helping me publish my book. God truly gifted you with a creative side that I lack. I pray that He continues to bless your business.

I'm thankful for Tim and Cindy Jines. You are warriors who faithfully stand with me during the toughest times. Thank you for never giving up hope and believing that God would heal me.

God placed a beautiful, faithful lady in my life that is like a second mom to me. Barbara Branscum, you truly inspire me to live life to the fullest and enjoy every minute of it.

My acknowledgments would not be complete without recognizing Jim and Debbie Sharp; you are friends that stood with me even when we were apart. God brought us back together at the perfect time, and I am grateful that He did. Your love, support, and ministry to me reflect God's light brightly. Continue to shine for Jesus!

Bibliography

Anderson, N. T. (2000). *Victory Over Darkness*. Ventura: Regal Books.

Barnes, A. (1962). *Barnes' Notes on the New Testament*. Grand Rapids: Kregel Publications.

Evans, T. (2015). *Victory in Spiritual Warfare*. Nashville: B&H Publishing.

Hagee, J. (2012, November 19). John Hagee Ministries. Retrieved from John Hagee Ministries: https://www.facebook.com/JohnHageeMinistries/

Hagin, K. E. (1999). *Bible Faith Study Course*. Tulsa: Kenneth Hagin Ministries.

Meyer, J. (2004). *Straight Talk*. New York: First Warner Books.

Osteen, D. (2003). *Healed of Cancer*. Houston: Thomas Nelson.

Walsh, S. (2004). *The Heartache No One Sees*. Nashville: Thomas Nelson.

Young, S. (2011). *Jesus Calling*. Nashville: Thomas Nelson.